Microsoft

Microsoft
OneNote
Step by Step

Curtis Frye

PUBLISHED BY
Microsoft Press
A division of Microsoft Corporation
One Microsoft Way
Redmond, Washington 98052-6399

Library of Congress Control Number: 2015938173
ISBN: 978-0-7356-9781-2

Printed and bound in the United States of America.

First Printing

Microsoft Press books are available through booksellers and distributors worldwide. If you need support related to this book, email Microsoft Press Support at mspinput@microsoft.com. Please tell us what you think of this book at http://aka.ms/tellpress.

This book is provided "as-is" and expresses the author's views and opinions. The views, opinions, and information expressed in this book, including URL and other Internet website references, may change without notice.

Some examples depicted herein are provided for illustration only and are fictitious. No real association or connection is intended or should be inferred.

Acquisitions Editor: Rosemary Caperton
Developmental Editor: Carol Dillingham
Editorial Production: Online Training Solutions, Inc. (OTSI)
Technical Reviewer: Ed Price
Copyeditor: Kathy Krause (OTSI)
Indexers: Susie Carr and Joan Lambert (OTSI)
Cover: Twist Creative • Seattle

For Virginia, my wife and love of my life.

Contents

Give us feedback
Tell us what you think of this book and help Microsoft improve our products for you. Thank you!
http://aka.ms/tellpress

Give us feedback
Tell us what you think of this book and help Microsoft
improve our products for you. Thank you!
http://aka.ms/tellpress

Introduction

Welcome! This *Step by Step* book has been designed so you can read it from the beginning to learn about Microsoft OneNote and then build your skills as you learn to perform increasingly specialized procedures. Or, if you prefer, you can jump in wherever you need ready guidance for performing tasks. The how-to steps are delivered crisply and concisely—just the facts. You'll also find informative, full-color graphics that support the instructional content.

Who this book is for

Microsoft OneNote Step by Step is designed for use as a learning and reference resource by home and business users of Microsoft Office apps who want to use OneNote to take and organize project notes; add images, shapes, and handwriting to notes; share notes with friends and colleagues; and embed Microsoft Excel spreadsheets in notes to manage data and create useful visualizations. The content of the book is designed to be useful for people who have previously used earlier versions of OneNote and for people who are discovering OneNote for the first time.

The *Step by Step* approach

The book's coverage is divided into chapters representing OneNote skill set areas, and each chapter is divided into topics that group related skills. Each topic includes expository information followed by generic procedures. At the end of the chapter, you'll find a series of practice tasks you can complete on your own by using the skills taught in the chapter. You can use the practice files that are available from this book's website to work through the practice tasks, or you can use your own files.

Download the practice files

Before you can complete the practice tasks in this book, you need to download the book's practice files to your computer from *http://aka.ms/OneNoteSBS/downloads*. Follow the instructions on the Downloads tab.

 IMPORTANT OneNote is not available from the book's website. You should install that app before working through the procedures and practice tasks in this book.

The practice file folder for each chapter includes a OneNote notebook (and sometimes additional practice files). Each notebook has a section for each set of practice tasks in that chapter. After you download the practice files, you can open the notebooks directly from the practice file folders, and close them after you complete the practice tasks.

 SEE ALSO For information about opening and closing notebooks, see "Create and manage OneNote notebooks" in Chapter 1, "Manage notebooks, sections, and pages."

OneNote automatically saves changes that you make to the notebooks. If you later want to repeat practice tasks, you can download the original practice files again.

The following table lists the practice files for this book.

Chapter	Folder	Notebooks and files
1: Manage notebooks, sections, and pages	Ch01	OneNoteSBS_Ch01
2: Create and format notes	Ch02	OneNoteSBS_Ch02
3: Work with your notes	Ch03	OneNoteSBS_Ch03 LevelDescriptions.docx WineryLandscape.jpg
4: Add ink and shapes to a notebook	Ch04	OneNoteSBS_Ch04
5: Review and password-protect notebook text	Ch05	OneNoteSBS_Ch05
6: Manage views, windows, and page versions	Ch06	OneNoteSBS_Ch06 LevelDescriptions.docx
7: Organize notes by using tags and categories	Ch07	OneNoteSBS_Ch07
8: Print and share notebooks and pages	Ch08	OneNoteSBS_Ch08
9: Use OneNote with Outlook and Excel	Ch09	OneNoteSBS_Ch09 IdentifyTrends.xlsx
10: Manage OneNote options and the interface	Ch10	None
11: Enhance OneNote by using the Onetastic add-in	Ch11	OneNoteSBS_Ch11

Ebook edition

If you're reading the ebook edition of this book, you can do the following:

- Search the full text
- Print
- Copy and paste

You can purchase and download the ebook edition from the Microsoft Press Store at *http://aka.ms/OneNoteSBS/details*.

Get support and give feedback

This topic provides information about getting help with this book and contacting us to provide feedback or report errors.

Errata and support

We've made every effort to ensure the accuracy of this book and its companion content. If you discover an error, please submit it to us at *http://aka.ms/OneNoteSBS /errata*.

If you need to contact the Microsoft Press Support team, please send an email message to *mspinput@microsoft.com*.

For help with Microsoft software and hardware, go to *http://support.microsoft.com*.

We want to hear from you

At Microsoft Press, your satisfaction is our top priority, and your feedback our most valuable asset. Please tell us what you think of this book at *http://aka.ms/tellpress*.

The survey is short, and we read every one of your comments and ideas. Thanks in advance for your input!

Stay in touch

Let's keep the conversation going! We're on Twitter at *http://twitter.com/MicrosoftPress*.

Adapt exercise steps

This book contains many images of the OneNote user interface elements (such as the ribbon and the app window) that you'll work with while performing tasks in OneNote on a Windows computer. Depending on your screen resolution or app window width, the OneNote ribbon on your screen might look different from the one shown in this book. As a result, procedural instructions that involve the ribbon might require a little adaptation.

Simple procedural instructions use this format:

1. On the **Insert** tab, in the **Time Stamp** group, click the **Time** button.

If the command is in a list, the instructions use this format:

1. On the **Draw** tab, in the **Edit** group, click the **Arrange** button and then, in the **Arrange** list, click **Bring Forward**.

If differences between your display settings and mine cause a button to appear differently on your screen than it does in this book, you can easily adapt the steps to locate the command. First click the specified tab, and then locate the specified group. If a group has been collapsed into a group list or under a group button, click the list or button to display the group's commands. If you can't immediately identify the button you want, point to likely candidates to display their names in ScreenTips.

Multistep procedural instructions use this format:

1. To select the images that you want to move forward, hold down the **Ctrl** key and click the images.

2. On the **Draw** tab, in the **Edit** group, click the **Arrange** button to display a menu of arrangement options.

3. On the **Arrange** menu, click **Bring Forward**.

On subsequent instances of instructions that require you to follow the same process, the instructions might be simplified in this format because the working location has already been established:

1. Select the images you want to move backward.

2. On the **Arrange** menu, click **Send Backward**.

The instructions in this book assume that you're interacting with on-screen elements on your computer by clicking (with a mouse, touchpad, or other hardware device). If you're using a different method—for example, if your computer has a touchscreen interface and you're tapping the screen (with your finger or a stylus)—substitute the applicable tapping action when you interact with a user interface element.

Instructions in this book refer to OneNote user interface elements that you click or tap on the screen as *buttons*, and to physical buttons that you press on a keyboard as *keys*, to conform to the standard terminology used in documentation for these products.

When the instructions tell you to enter information, you can do so by typing on a connected external keyboard, tapping an on-screen keyboard, or even speaking aloud, depending on your computer setup and your personal preferences.

Manage notebooks, sections, and pages

When you start the OneNote app, it displays the last notebook you had open or, if you start OneNote without having created a notebook, it creates a new one for you. Either way, OneNote makes it easy to create and keep track of all your notebooks.

Each new notebook contains one section (represented as a tab on the navigation bar), which in turn contains one page. Just as you can create and manage notebooks, you can also organize your notes by creating, moving, or even deleting sections and pages. Sections help you organize your notes by subject, whereas pages give you a finer level of control over your notebook's organization. You can copy, move, and reorder sections and pages, and you can even create section groups if your notebook starts to get a bit crowded.

This chapter guides you through procedures related to creating and managing OneNote notebooks, creating and managing notebook sections, and creating and managing notebook pages.

In this chapter

- Create and manage OneNote notebooks
- Create and manage notebook sections
- Create and manage notebook pages

Practice files

For this chapter, use the practice files from the OneNoteSBS\Ch01 folder. For practice file download instructions, see the introduction.

Create and manage OneNote notebooks

A OneNote notebook provides a central structure for notes you capture within the app. As with other types of files, you can copy, move, rename, and delete notebook files by using File Explorer. One significant difference between OneNote notebooks and other files is that a notebook is stored as a folder.

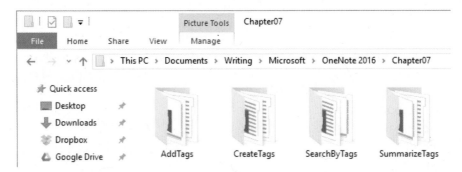

OneNote notebooks are stored as folders

When you double-click the folder in File Explorer, you see a set of files that represent the notebook's contents—specifically, a file for each notebook section and a file named Open Notebook.

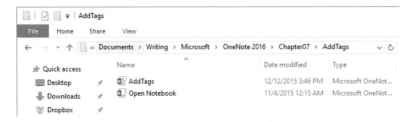

Each section is represented as a file within the notebook folder

If you double-click a section file, OneNote opens the notebook and displays that section. If you double-click the Open Notebook file, OneNote opens the notebook and displays the page that was active when you closed the notebook.

You can store notebooks on your computer, on storage devices available through your local network, and in Microsoft OneDrive directories, SharePoint libraries, and other online storage locations. You can open a notebook from any device that has access to the storage location.

> **IMPORTANT** Renaming a notebook can cause it to lose its connection to other copies of the notebook on OneDrive, SharePoint, or other computers. To prevent such errors from happening, you should avoid renaming notebooks.

To create a new notebook on OneDrive

1. In OneNote, click the **File** tab of the ribbon to display the Backstage view.

2. In the left pane of the Backstage view, click **New** to display the New page.

3. If necessary, click **OneDrive**. If you have multiple OneDrive options, select the appropriate one.

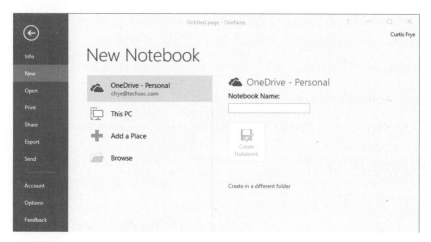

Create a new notebook from the Backstage view

4. In the **Notebook Name** box, enter a name for the new notebook.

5. Do either of the following:

   - Click the **Create Notebook** button to create the notebook in the current OneDrive folder.

   - Click the **Create in a different folder** link. Then in the **Create New Notebook** dialog box, navigate to the OneDrive folder where you want to create the new notebook, and click **Create**.

6. In the confirmation dialog box that opens, click **Invite People** to give colleagues access to the file, or click **Not Now** to create the notebook without sharing it.

To create a new notebook on your computer

1. In OneNote, on the **New** page of the Backstage view, click **This PC**.

2. In the **Notebook Name** box, enter a name for the new notebook.

3. Click **Create Notebook**.

Or

1. On the **New** page of the Backstage view, click **This PC**.

2. In the **Notebook Name** box, enter a name for the new notebook.

3. Click **Create in a different folder**.

4. In the **Create New Notebook** dialog box, navigate to the folder where you want to create the new notebook.

5. Click **Create**.

To open a notebook stored on your computer

1. In OneNote, do either of the following to display the Open page of the Backstage view:

    •   In the left pane of the Backstage view, click **Open**.

    •   Press **Ctrl+O**.

2. On the **Open** page of the Backstage view, click **This PC**.

Navigate to the folder that contains the file you want to open

3. Use the tools in the right pane of the **Open from other locations** section of the page to navigate to the folder that contains the notebook you want to open.

4. Click the notebook to open it.

TIP Right-clicking a notebook displays options to open it, to copy the path, to pin it to (or unpin it from) the Recent list, to remove it from the list, or to unpin all the items.

To open a notebook stored on OneDrive

1. Display the **Open** page of the Backstage view.

2. In the **Open from OneDrive** section, in the **My Notebooks** list, double-click the notebook you want to open.

> **TIP** If all of your OneDrive notebooks are already open in OneNote, the app displays a message indicating that fact. You can click the Manage Notebooks On OneDrive link to open OneDrive in your web browser.

Or

1. Display the **Open** page of the Backstage view.

2. In the **Open from other locations** section, use the tools in the navigation pane to display the OneDrive folder that contains the notebook you want to open.

3. Click the notebook to open it.

To open a recently accessed notebook

1. Display the **Open** page of the Backstage view.

2. In the **Open from other locations** section, click **Recent**.

3. In the **Recent** list in the right pane, click the notebook you want to open.

To open a notebook from within File Explorer

1. In File Explorer, navigate to the folder that contains the notebook you want to open.

2. Double-click the folder that represents the notebook you want to open.

3. Double-click the **Open Notebook** file.

To close a notebook

1. Above the notebook page, to the left of the section tabs, do either of the following:

    - Right-click the active notebook name, and then click **Close This Notebook**.

    - Click the active notebook name to display a list of open notebooks. Right-click the notebook you want to close, and then click **Close This Notebook**.

Create and manage notebook sections

OneNote notebooks provide the basic structure for managing your thoughts on a variety of subjects, but storing notes on multiple topics in a single group can be confusing. If you plan to keep notes on several subjects in the same notebook, you should create a distinct section for each topic.

A section provides a level of organization within a notebook that corresponds well to individual projects or subjects. Just as a physical three-ring binder works best when divided into sections, so does a OneNote notebook. After you create a section, you can display its contents, rename it, copy or move it to another notebook (or within the current notebook), or export it to another format, such as a PDF, Word document, or as a copy of the OneNote file that you want to save. You can also make a section's tab stand out by changing its tab color.

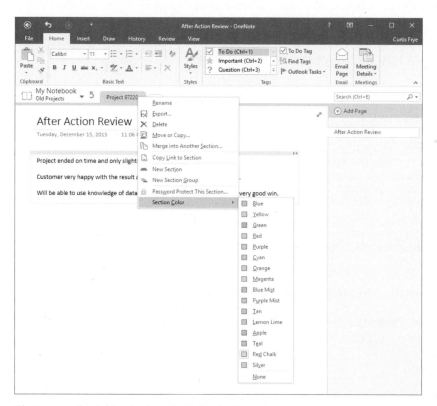

Change a section tab's color to make it stand out

If you find that you've created too many sections and want to merge two of them into a single section, you can do so quickly and choose whether or not to delete the original section. You can also add another level of organization by creating a section group in your notebook. Just as a section contains one or more pages, a section group contains one or more sections. When the section group is open, the navigation bar includes a curved arrow button that, when clicked, returns you to the top level of organization within the notebook.

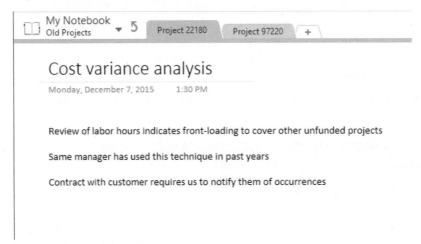

Add a level of organization by creating a section group

To create a new section tab to the right of the notebook's sections

1. Do either of the following:

   - To the right of the section tabs, above the active notebook page, click the **Create a New Section** button (the tab with the plus sign).

   - Press **Ctrl+T**.

To insert a new section to the right of an existing section

1. Right-click the tab of the section you want to insert the new section after, and then click **New Section**.

To display a section

1. In the section tabs above the active notebook page, click the tab of the section you want to display.

To rename a section

1. In the section tabs above the active notebook page, right-click the tab of the section you want to rename, and then click **Rename**.

>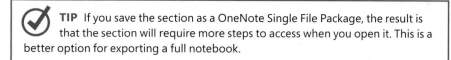
> **TIP** You can also double-click the section tab to select the section's name.

2. Enter a new name for the section.

3. Press **Enter**.

To export a section as a separate file

1. In the tabs above the active notebook page, right-click the tab of the section you want to export, and then click **Export**.

2. In the **Save As** dialog box, navigate to the folder to which you want to export the section.

3. In the **File name** box, enter a name for the exported file.

4. Click the **Save as type** arrow, and then do one of the following:

   - Select the default **OneNote Section** to save a copy of the section file to a new location.

   > **TIP** If you save the section as a OneNote Single File Package, the result is that the section will require more steps to access when you open it. This is a better option for exporting a full notebook.

   - Select **Single File Web Page** if you plan to upload the section online as a webpage.

   - Select **PDF** to create a version that is ready for printing and not easily edited.

   - Select **XPS Document** as an alternative for printing.

   - Select **Microsoft Word XML Document** if you use Word 2007 or later and want to have or share an editable document.

   - Select **Microsoft Word Document** if you use an older version of Word or prefer the file type for other reasons.

5. Click **Save**.

To copy a section within a notebook

1. Right-click the tab of the section you want to copy, and then click **Move or Copy**.

2. In the **Move or Copy Section** dialog box, click the show detail button (the plus sign) next to the current notebook to expand the section list.

3. Click the section to the left of where you want the copied section to appear.

4. Click **Copy**.

Or

1. Hold down the **Ctrl** key, and drag the tab of the section you want to copy to a new location among the section tabs.

 TIP You won't be able to export a section if you're viewing it in OneNote Open Sections, because that is a grouping of temporarily open sections. You can copy those sections into a notebook for more control and to keep a copy of the content.

To move a section within a notebook

1. In the section tabs above the active notebook page, drag the tab of the section you want to move to its new location.

 TIP A small black triangle indicates where the section tab will be placed within the notebook.

Or

1. Right-click the tab of the section you want to move, and then click **Move or Copy**.

2. In the **Move or Copy Section** dialog box, click the show detail button (the plus sign) next to the current notebook to expand the section list.

3. Click the section to the left of where you want the section to be moved.

4. Click **Move**.

To copy a section to another notebook

1. Right-click the tab of the section you want to copy to another notebook, and then click **Move or Copy**.

2. In the **Move or Copy Section** dialog box, do either of the following:

   • Click the notebook to which you want to copy the section. This places the copied section at the end (the far right) of the tabs in the target notebook.

   • Click the show detail button (the plus sign) to display the sections in the target notebook, and then click the section you want the copied section to appear after in the target notebook.

3. Click **Copy**.

To move a section to another notebook

1. Right-click the tab of the section you want to move to another notebook, and then click **Move or Copy**.

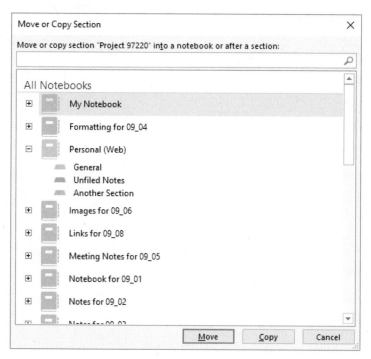

Move a section to another notebook

2. In the **Move or Copy Section** dialog box, do either of the following:

    - Click the notebook to which you want to move the section. This places the moved section at the end (the far right) of the tabs in the target notebook.

    - Click the show detail button (the plus sign) to display the sections in the target notebook, and then click the section you want the moved section to appear after in the target notebook.

3. Click **Move**.

Or

1. At the top of the app window, to the left of the section tabs, click the **Click to view other notebooks** arrow to display a list of other notebooks.

2. At the top of the list, in the upper-right corner, click the **Pin Notebook Pane to Side** button (the pushpin). The list of other notebooks is opened in its own pane on the left side of the app window.

3. In the notebooks list, click the **Expand** arrow to the right of the notebook from which you want to move a section, to display the sections in that notebook.

4. Click the **Expand** arrow to the right of the notebook to which you want to move the section.

5. Drag the section you want to move from the source notebook to the target notebook.

To change the color of a section tab

1. Right-click the section tab you want to change, point to **Section Color**, and then click the color you want to apply.

To merge sections

1. Right-click the tab of the section you want to merge with another section, and then click **Merge into Another Section**.

2. In the **Merge Section** dialog box, click the show detail button (the plus sign) to show the sections within the target notebook.

3. Click the section into which you want to merge the selected section.

1

4. Click **Merge**.

5. In the first **Microsoft OneNote** confirmation dialog box that opens, confirm your decision by clicking **Merge Sections**.

6. If you want to delete the original tab (a full merge), in the second **Microsoft OneNote** dialog box, click **Delete**. Otherwise, click **No**.

 TIP The merged pages appear below any existing pages in the section they were merged into. They are in the same order as they were in the original section.

To delete a section

1. Right-click the tab of the section you want to delete, and then click **Delete**.

2. In the confirmation dialog box that opens, click **Yes**.

To create a section group

1. Right-click any section tab, and then click **New Section Group**.

2. Enter the section group name, while the group tab's title **New Section Group** is highlighted.

 TIP To move, copy, and delete sections within or among section groups, display the section groups and follow the steps described elsewhere in this procedure set.

To display a section group

1. To the right of the section tabs above the notebook page, click the tab of the section group you want to display.

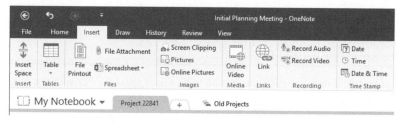

Click the tab representing a section group to display the sections it contains

To exit a section group

1. To the left of the section tabs above the notebook page, click the **Navigate to parent section group** button (an arrowed line curving counterclockwise).

To save a section before deleting its group

1. In the section group that you are going to delete, right-click the tab of the section that you want to save, and click **Move or Copy**. Use the **Move or Copy Section** dialog box to move your section, as described earlier in these procedures.

Or

1. At the top of the app window, to the left of the section tabs, click the **Click to view other notebooks** arrow to display a list of other notebooks.

2. At the top of the list, in the upper-right corner, click the **Pin Notebook Pane to Side** button (the pushpin). The list of other notebooks is opened in its own pane on the left side of the app window.

3. In the notebooks list, click the **Expand** arrow to the right of the notebook from which you are going to delete the section group, to display the sections in that notebook. If necessary, click the name of the section group to display the sections within it.

4. If necessary, click the **Expand** arrow to the right of the notebook to which you want to move the section, if you're going to move the section into a different notebook.

5. Drag the section you want to move from your section group into another placement in the same notebook or another expanded notebook.

To delete a section group and its pages

1. Right-click the section group header, and then click **Delete**.

2. In the confirmation dialog box that opens, click **Yes**.

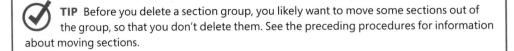

TIP Before you delete a section group, you likely want to move some sections out of the group, so that you don't delete them. See the preceding procedures for information about moving sections.

Create and manage notebook pages

The lowest level of organization within a OneNote notebook is the page, which contains the notes, images, and other elements you capture and create to help you with your work.

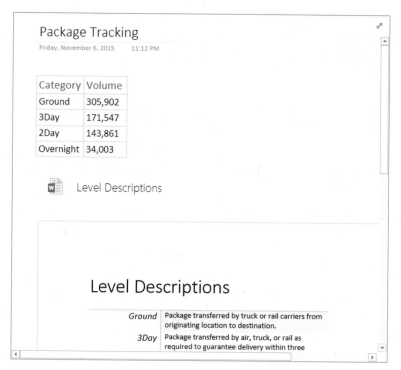

Notebook pages contain information about your projects, such as tables of data and linked files

A new notebook includes one section and one untitled page. You can give the page a title, or change its existing title, by entering its text on the title line, which is just above the text that lists the date and time when you created the page. If you copied a page from another notebook, or if you want to use a different starting point for a page, you can change the page date and time.

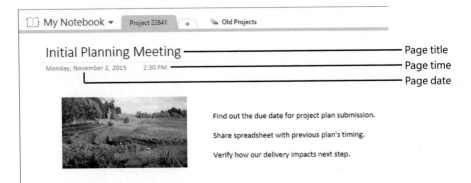

Pages include editable titles, dates, and times

As with sections in a notebook, you can copy and move individual pages, either within the current notebook or to another notebook. OneNote provides a visual indicator showing where a page will appear after you move it, so you can make your changes with confidence.

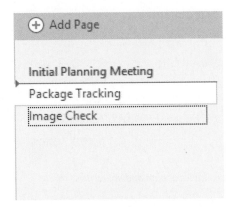

Move a page within a OneNote notebook

To create a new page

1. Do any of the following:

    -   In the section where you want to create the new page, click the **Add Page** button at the top of the page tab pane on the right.

    -   Press **Ctrl+N**.

    -   Point to any tab that represents an existing page. When the insert page indicator appears (it looks like a right-pointing polygon with a plus sign inside it), click the indicator to insert the page.

2. Enter the page name (your cursor starts in the title section of the new page), and press **Enter**.

To change the date displayed below the page title

1. Click the date text displayed below the page title.

2. Click the calendar icon.

3. Use the calendar control to select a new day.

To change the time displayed below the page title

1. Click the time value displayed below the page title.

2. Click the clock icon.

3. In the **Change Page Time** dialog box, click the **Page time** list arrow, and then click a time.

    > **TIP** Because the default time is set to the current time, if you click OK without changing anything, the time is updated to the current time. Make sure you click Cancel if you don't want to change the time.

4. Click **OK**.

To rename a page

1. Edit the page's title text on the notebook page.

To copy a page within a section

1. In the page tab pane on the right, hold down the **Ctrl** key and drag the page to a new location in the pane.

Or

1. Right-click the page tab, and then click **Move or Copy**.

2. In the **Move or Copy Pages** dialog box, click the show detail button (the plus sign) next to the current notebook.

3. Click the section into which you want to copy the page. The page is copied below any other pages in the new section.

4. Click **Copy**.

To move a page within a section

1. In the page tab pane on the right, drag the page to a new location in the pane.

To copy a page to another section in the same notebook

1. In the page tab pane, hold down the **Ctrl** key and drag the page up to the section tabs above the current page.

2. When the pointer is over the tab of the target section, release the mouse button.

To move a page to another section in the same notebook

1. In the page tab pane, drag the page up to the section tabs above the current page.

2. When the pointer is over the tab of the target section, release the mouse button.

To copy a page to a different notebook

1. Right-click the tab of the page you want to copy, and then click **Move or Copy**.

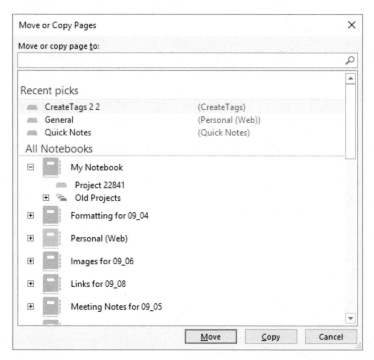

Copy a page to another notebook

2. In the **Move or Copy Pages** dialog box, click the show detail button (the plus sign) to show the sections in the target notebook.

3. Click the section where you want the copied page to appear in the target notebook.

4. Click **Copy**.

Or

1. At the top of the app window, to the left of the section tabs, click the **Click to view other notebooks** arrow to display a list of other notebooks.

2. At the top of the list, in the upper-right corner, click the **Pin Notebook Pane to Side** button (the pushpin). The list of other notebooks is opened in its own pane on the left side of the app window.

3. In the notebooks list, click the **Expand** arrow to the right of the notebook to which you want to copy the page, to display the sections in that notebook.

4. While holding down the **Ctrl** key, drag the page tab from the page tab pane to the **Notebooks** pane on the left.

5. When the pointer is over the name of the section into which you want to copy the page, do either of the following:

    -   Release the mouse button to add a copy of the page at the bottom of that section.

    -   Pause over the section until the app window changes to display the pages for the target section. Move the pointer to the page tab pane for the target section until it points to where you want to insert the copy, and then release the mouse button to insert the copy between the existing pages.

To move a page to a different notebook

1. Right-click the tab of the page you want to move to another notebook, and then click **Move or Copy**.

2. In the **Move or Copy Pages** dialog box, click the show detail button (the plus sign), to show the sections in the target notebook.

3. Click the section you want to move the page to.

4. Click **Move**.

Or

1. At the top of the app window, to the left of the section tabs, click the **Click to view other notebooks** arrow to display a list of other notebooks.

2. At the top of the list, in the upper-right corner, click the **Pin Notebook Pane to Side** button (the pushpin). The list of other notebooks is opened in its own pane on the left side of the app window.

3. In the notebooks list, click the **Expand** arrow to the right of the notebook to which you want to move the page, to display the sections in that notebook.

4. Drag the page tab from the page tab pane to the **Notebooks** pane on the left.

5. When the pointer is over the name of the section into which you want to move the page, do either of the following:

- Release the mouse button to move the page to the bottom of that section.

- Pause over the section until the app window changes to display the pages for the target section. Move the pointer to the page tab pane for the target section until it points to where you want to move the page, and then release the mouse button to insert the page between the existing pages.

To delete a page

1. Click the page tab to select the page.

2. Do any of the following:

- On the **Home** tab, in the **Basic Text** group, click the **Delete** button.

- Press the **Delete** key.

- Press the **Backspace** key.

Or

1. Right-click the page tab, and then click **Delete**.

Skills review

In this chapter, you learned how to:

- Create and manage OneNote notebooks

- Create and manage notebook sections

- Create and manage notebook pages

Practice tasks

The practice files for these tasks are located in the OneNoteSBS\Ch01 folder. The results of the tasks will be automatically saved into the same file in the same folder.

Create and manage OneNote notebooks

Start OneNote, and then perform the following tasks:

1. Create a new notebook named **NextProjects** on your computer.

2. Exit OneNote.

3. Display the **NextProjects** notebook in File Explorer, and then double-click its folder to display the folder's contents.

4. Double-click **Open Notebook** to reopen the NextProjects notebook.

Create and manage notebook sections

Open the ManageSections section in OneNote, and then perform the following tasks:

1. Create a new section named **Project 97220**.

2. Change the **Project 97220** section's tab color to **Teal**.

3. Create a new section group named **Completed Projects**.

4. Move the **Project 97220** section into the **Completed Projects** group.

Create and manage notebook pages

Open the ManagePages section in OneNote, and then perform the following tasks:

1. Create a new page named **Project 13214**.

2. Move the page to the top of the page list so it's first in the page order.

3. Change the date and time of the **Project 13214** page to **9:00 AM** on your birthday.

Create and format notes

2

OneNote notebooks give you the tools you need to record, organize, and build on your thoughts. After you create a notebook, you can start adding notes. The most direct way to start adding notes is to click anywhere on the active page and start typing. After you add your notes, you can move them to another location, copy all or part of a note, and change the formatting as needed.

You can use formatting within OneNote to create headers that identify notes on a particular topic, emphasize text by using bold or italic formatting, and highlight text to group thoughts visually even when they're on different parts of a page.

This chapter guides you through procedures related to creating, cutting, and copying notes; applying text formatting to notes; creating lists and outlines; changing paragraph formatting; and deleting formatting and items.

In this chapter

- Create, cut, and copy notes
- Apply text formatting to notes
- Create lists and outlines
- Change paragraph formatting
- Delete formatting and items

Practice files

For this chapter, use the practice files from the OneNoteSBS\Ch02 folder. For practice file download instructions, see the introduction.

Create, cut, and copy notes

There are two main ways to enter notes into OneNote: by using a keyboard, or by writing or drawing with your finger or other input device on a touch-sensitive screen. This chapter focuses on input and formatting that use the keyboard and mouse.

 TIP Touchscreen entry is referred to as *ink entry mode*, or sometimes just *ink*. For information about adding ink input to a OneNote notebook, see Chapter 4, "Add ink and shapes to a notebook."

You can start adding typed notes to a OneNote page by clicking the spot on the page where you want the notes to begin and entering text by using the keyboard. After you have entered a note, you can move or copy the note as a whole, select and copy or cut text from the note, or delete the note entirely.

 TIP OneNote stores cut or copied items in the Clipboard, from which you can paste the item into your notebook.

After you cut or copy an item, or text from within an item, you can control how OneNote pastes those contents into your notebook. You can keep the original formatting, merge the formatting from the original item and the destination item, paste text only, or paste an image of the item you copied to the Clipboard.

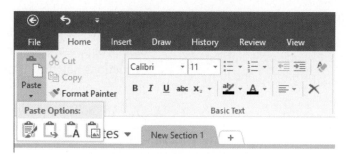

Control how you paste copied items into a notebook

2

To create a note

1. Click within the page where you want to create your note.

2. Do either of the following:

   - Use the keyboard to enter the text you want.

   - Use a stylus to enter the text you want.

 TIP Clicking in a different place on the same page starts a new note.

To reposition a note

1. Point to the gray horizontal bar at the top of the note. The pointer is in position when it turns into a four-headed arrow.

2. Drag the note to a new location.

To copy a note

1. Click the gray horizontal bar at the top of the note.

2. Do any of the following:

   - On the **Home** tab of the ribbon, in the **Clipboard** group, click **Copy**.

   - Press **Ctrl+C**.

   - Right-click the note, and then click **Copy**.

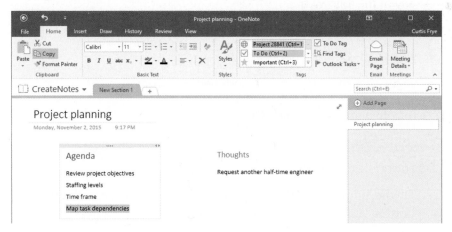

Select and copy note text to reuse content in OneNote

To cut a note

1. Click the title bar of the note.

2. Do any of the following:

   - On the **Home** tab of the ribbon, in the **Clipboard** group, click the **Cut** button.

   - Press **Ctrl+X**.

   - Right-click the note, and click **Cut**.

To delete a note without saving it to the Clipboard

1. Click the title bar of the note.

2. Do any of the following:

   - On the **Home** tab of the ribbon, in the **Basic Text** group, click the **Delete** button.

   - Press the **Delete** key.

   - Right-click the note, and then click **Delete**.

To copy text from a note to the Clipboard

1. Select the text you want to copy.

2. Do any of the following:

   - On the **Home** tab of the ribbon, in the **Clipboard** group, click **Copy**.

   - Press **Ctrl+C**.

   - Right-click the selected text, and then click **Copy**.

To cut text from a note and save it to the Clipboard

1. Select the text you want to cut.

2. Do any of the following:

   - On the **Home** tab of the ribbon, in the **Clipboard** group, click the **Cut** button.

   - Press **Ctrl+X**.

   - Right-click the selected text, and then click **Cut**.

To paste text into a note

1. Cut or copy text to the Clipboard.

2. Click within your note so the cursor appears at the location where you want the pasted text to appear.

3. Do either of the following:

   - On the **Home** tab of the ribbon, in the **Clipboard** group, click the **Paste** button.

   - Press **Ctrl+V**.

To paste text as a new note

1. Cut or copy text to the Clipboard.

2. Click a blank spot on the page to create a new note.

3. Do either of the following:

   - On the **Home** tab of the ribbon, click the **Paste** button.

   - Press **Ctrl+V**.

To paste text by using Paste Options

1. Cut or copy text to the Clipboard.

2. Do either of the following:

   - Position the cursor within an existing note.

   - Click a blank spot on a page to create a new note.

3. Do either of the following:

   - On the **Home** tab of the ribbon, in the **Clipboard** group, click the **Paste** arrow, and then click the icon representing the paste option you want to apply.

   - Right-click the paste destination and then, under **Paste Options**, click the icon representing the option you want to apply.

Apply text formatting to notes

You'll find the editing and formatting controls, which let you change the text's appearance, to be very familiar if you've worked with other Microsoft Office apps, such as Word or PowerPoint.

Use the controls on the Home tab of the ribbon to format your notes

By default, OneNote creates text by using the Calibri font, with its size set to 11 points. (There are 72 points to an inch.) You can use any font installed on your system to format your text according to your needs. You might want to use one font for your basic note text and another for headlines, for example.

Applying bold, italic, and underline formatting all emphasize the text you formatted, but in slightly different ways. For example, bold text can identify a key term, italics can denote a definition of that term, and underlining can indicate vital words within the definition that help distinguish the term from related concepts. For more specific cases, such as mathematical notes or to indicate a word that should be excluded from a definition, you can apply subscript, superscript, or strikethrough formatting.

> ⚠️ **IMPORTANT** The uses for bold, italic, and underline formatting mentioned previously are just suggestions. Use the scheme that makes the most sense for each item in your notebook's context.

Another way to make text stand out on the page is to apply highlighting, which is the electronic equivalent of using a light-colored marker to distinguish text on a printed page. You can also change the color of specific text. In most cases, the standard black text is best, but red text can identify mistakes to avoid, and green text can indicate action items, or whatever combination works best for you.

> **TIP** When you first select an entire note or just the text you want to format, OneNote opens a Mini Toolbar that includes most of the buttons from the Basic Text group of the Home tab. This is so you can make your formatting changes as quickly and easily as possible. The toolbar also includes some buttons from the Styles and Tags groups.

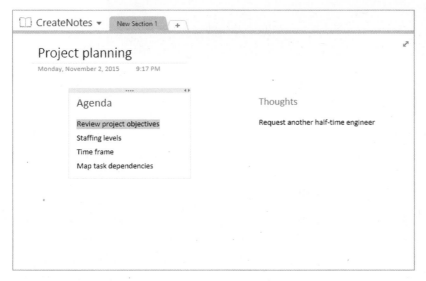

Highlight text to make it stand out from surrounding information

Finally, meetings and classes often cover several topics during each session. You can use the built-in styles to apply several levels of headings to your notes, call out citations and quotes, or format programming code so it's easier to distinguish from the surrounding text.

> **TIP** Depending on how comprehensive a note-taker you are, you might want to wait until the pace of your class or meeting slows down before adding heading and other styles. If necessary, you could wait to apply the formatting when you review your notes after the class or meeting.

To change the font of text

1. Select the text you want to format.

2. On the **Home** tab of the ribbon, in the **Basic Text** group, click the **Font** arrow.

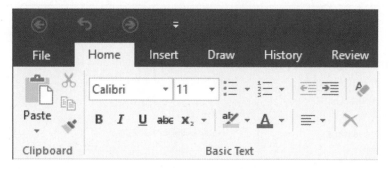

Format text by using the tools in the Home tab's Basic Text group

3. Click the font you want to apply.

> **TIP** You can click within the Font text box and start typing the name of a font. OneNote displays the first font that starts with those characters. When you click the Font arrow, the Font list opens, with the font name highlighted in the Font text box at the bottom of your view of the Font list.

To change the size of text

1. Select the text you want to format.

2. Do either of the following:

   - On the **Home** tab of the ribbon, in the **Basic Text** group, click the **Font Size** arrow and select the size you want to apply.

   - Click in the **Font Size** text box, enter the font size you want to apply, and press **Enter**.

To apply bold formatting to text

1. Select the text you want to format.

2. Do either of the following:

   - On the **Home** tab of the ribbon, in the **Basic Text** group, click the **Bold** button.

   - Press **Ctrl+B**.

Add bold formatting to make text stand out

To apply italic formatting to text

1. Select the text you want to format.

2. Do either of the following:

   - On the **Home** tab of the ribbon, in the **Basic Text** group, click the **Italic** button.

   - Press **Ctrl+I**.

To apply underline formatting to text

1. Select the text you want to format.

2. Do either of the following:

   - On the **Home** tab of the ribbon, in the **Basic Text** group, click the **Underline** button.

   - Press **Ctrl+U**.

To apply strikethrough formatting to text

1. Select the text you want to format.

2. On the **Home** tab of the ribbon, in the **Basic Text** group, click the **Strikethrough** button.

Use strikethrough formatting to leave text in place but indicate that it should be ignored

To apply subscript formatting to text

1. Select the text you want to format.

2. On the **Home** tab of the ribbon, in the **Basic Text** group, click the **Subscript** button.

To apply superscript formatting to text

1. Select the text you want to format.

2. On the **Home** tab of the ribbon, in the **Basic Text** group, click the **Subscript** arrow, and then click **Superscript**. (This button then stays on Superscript by default until you switch back.)

To highlight text

1. Select the text you want to format.

2. Do either of the following:

   - On the **Home** tab of the ribbon, in the **Basic Text** group, click the **Text Highlight Color** button to apply the last highlight color selected.

   - Click the **Text Highlight Color** arrow, and then click the highlight color you want to apply.

2

To change the font color of text

1. Select the text you want to format.

2. Do either of the following:

   - On the **Home** tab of the ribbon, in the **Basic Text** group, click the **Font Color** button to apply the last font color selected.

   - Click the **Font Color** arrow, and then click the font color you want to apply.

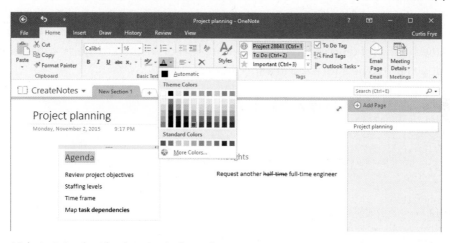

Make text stand out by changing its font color

To copy formatting from one item to another item

1. Select the text from which you want to copy formatting.

2. On the **Home** tab of the ribbon, in the **Clipboard** group, click the **Format Painter** button.

3. Select the text to which you want to apply the copied formatting.

To copy formatting from one item to multiple items

1. Select the text from which you want to copy formatting.

2. On the **Home** tab of the ribbon, in the **Clipboard** group, double-click the **Format Painter** button.

3. Select the first item to which you want to apply the copied formatting, and then select the other items you want to reformat, one at a time.

4. When you are done applying the copied formatting, press **Esc** to release the Format Painter.

Create lists and outlines

Managing meeting agendas, work tasks, and school assignments can be much easier if you create lists. It can be tempting to think that you will remember everything you need to do, but new tasks come up frequently, and it's likely that you will need a list to keep track of it all.

You can use OneNote to create two types of lists: numbered lists and bulleted lists. A numbered list is used for ideas or tasks that have an inherent order, such as a meeting agenda or steps in a process. Bulleted list items aren't numbered; the tasks or thoughts contained in the list represent distinct tasks or concepts related to the list's theme, but they don't have to be addressed in a specific order.

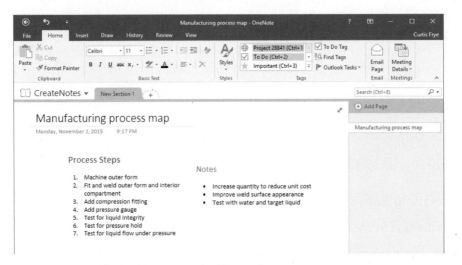

Use numbered and bulleted lists to organize ideas and processes

When you create a numbered or bulleted list, you can put items on different levels. For example, if you want to discuss the manufacturing process for a specific product, you could define second-level items that relate to the product.

Process Steps

1. Machine outer form
2. Fit and weld outer form and interior compartment
3. Add compression fitting
4. Add pressure gauge
5. Test for liquid integrity
   a. Test for pressure hold
   b. Test for liquid flow under pressure

A numbered list with two second-level items

OneNote also lets you move items within a list and from one list to another. By dragging an item up or down to change its position, or to the left or right to change its level within a list, you can alter your list so it reflects your evolving understanding of a task or subject. You can also drag an item to another list, without the need to cut and paste the item's text to another list.

After you create a list with differing levels, you can show or hide levels of detail within the outline you created or select every item at a particular level within the outline.

To create a list

1. Click a blank spot on a page to create an item.

2. Enter a list item, and then press **Enter**.

3. Repeat step 2 until your list is complete.

To create a numbered list

1. Create a list.

2. Select the list text.

3. On the **Home** tab of the ribbon, in the **Basic Text** group, click the **Numbering** button.

Or

1. Do any of the following to start a numbered list:

   - On the **Home** tab of the ribbon, in the **Basic Text** group, click the **Numbering** button.

   - Type 1., followed by a space.

   - Press **Ctrl+/.**

2. Enter a list item, and then press **Enter**.

3. Repeat step 2 until your list is complete.

To create a bulleted list

1. Create a list.

2. Select the list text.

3. On the **Home** tab of the ribbon, in the **Basic Text** group, click the **Bullets** button.

Or

1. Do any of the following to start a bulleted list:

   - On the **Home** tab of the ribbon, in the **Basic Text** group, click the **Bullets** button.

   - Enter * (an asterisk) followed by a space.

   - Enter - (a hyphen) followed by a space to use the dashed bullet style.

   - Press **Ctrl+.** (period).

2. Enter a list item, and then press **Enter**.

3. Repeat step 2 until your list is complete.

To change the numbering scheme of a numbered list

1. Select the text in your numbered list.

2. On the **Home** tab of the ribbon, in the **Basic Text** group, click the **Numbering** arrow, and then click the numbering scheme you want to apply.

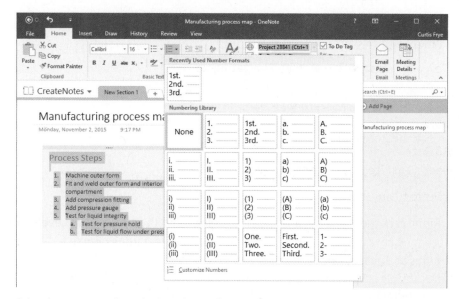

Select from a range of numbering schemes for a numbered list

To change the bullets of a bulleted list

1. Select the text in your bulleted list.

2. On the **Home** tab of the ribbon, in the **Basic Text** group, click the **Bullets** arrow, and then click the bulleting scheme you want to apply.

To select a list item

1. Point to the list item to display its item indicator.

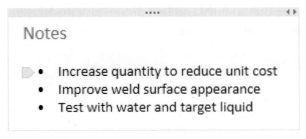

Click a list item's indicator to select it

2. Click the item indicator.

To select all list items at a specific level

1. Point to any item in the list.

2. Right-click the item indicator, point to **Select**, and then click **All at Level** #, where # represents the level of the items you want to select (for example, *2*). All of the items at that level are now selected.

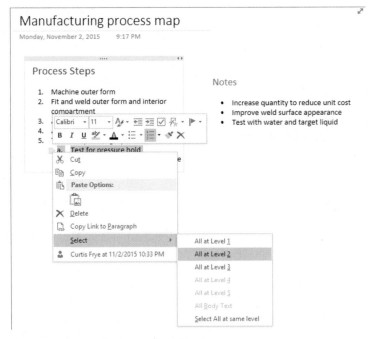

Select all items at a specific level within a list

To move an item within a list or to another list

1. Click anywhere in the text of the item you want to move.

2. Point to the list item. When the item indicator appears, drag the indicator down or up the list, until the item moves to its new place within the list.

To move an item down one level in a list

1. Click anywhere in the text of the item you want to move.

2. Perform any of the following steps:

   - On the **Home** tab of the ribbon, in the **Basic Text** group, click the **Increase Indent Position** button.

   - Point to the list item. When the item indicator appears, drag the indicator to the right until the item moves to its new level within the list.

   - Press **Alt+Shift+Right Arrow**.

To move an item up one level in a list

1. Click anywhere in the text of the item you want to move.

2. Perform any of the following steps:

   - On the **Home** tab of the ribbon, in the **Basic Text** group, click the **Decrease Indent Position** button.

   - Point to the list item. When the item indicator appears, drag the indicator to the left until the item moves to its new level within the list.

   - Press **Alt+Shift+Left Arrow**.

To hide a level of detail in a list

1. Double-click the item indicator above the lower-level items you want to hide.

To show a level of detail in a list

1. Double-click the **Show Detail** button (a plus symbol in a box) to the left of the item above the hidden lower-level items.

Change paragraph formatting

Just as you can apply formatting to individual items or sections of text, you can also format paragraphs by changing a paragraph's alignment or by increasing or decreasing the text's indentation. One common way to emphasize a quote, for example, is to indent the quote's text so it stands out from the surrounding text. You can also change your text's alignment so it aligns with the left, center, or right edge of the note it's contained within.

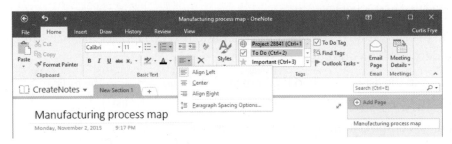

Select an alignment that fits a paragraph's role on the page

If you find your text is hard to read, perhaps because the lines are too close together, you can add space above or below a line, or set a minimum space between lines.

To change paragraph alignment

1. Do either of the following:

    - Click anywhere in the paragraph you want to align.

    - Select the paragraphs you want to align.

2. On the **Home** tab of the ribbon, in the **Basic Text** group, click the **Paragraph Alignment** button, and then click the alignment you want to apply.

To increase a paragraph's indent level

1. Do either of the following:

    - Click anywhere in the paragraph you want to format.

    - Select the paragraphs you want to format.

2. On the **Home** tab of the ribbon, in the **Basic Text** group, click the **Increase Indent Position** button.

To decrease a paragraph's indent level

1. Do either of the following:

   - Click anywhere in the paragraph you want to format.

   - Select the paragraphs you want to format.

2. On the **Home** tab of the ribbon, in the **Basic Text** group, click the **Decrease Indent Position** button.

To set paragraph spacing

1. Do either of the following:

   - Click anywhere in the paragraph you want to format.

   - Select the paragraphs you want to format.

2. On the **Home** tab of the ribbon, in the **Basic Text** group, click the **Paragraph Alignment** button, and then click **Paragraph Spacing Options**.

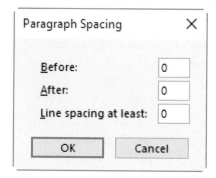

Control white space within and around paragraphs

3. In the **Paragraph Spacing** dialog box, do any of the following:

   - In the **Before** box, enter the number of points of blank space you want to have above the paragraph.

   - In the **After** box, enter the number of points of blank space you want to have below the paragraph.

   - In the **Line spacing at least** box, enter the minimum number of points of vertical space the line must occupy. This value includes the space above the line, the font size of the line, and the space below the line, so the results will differ depending on the font type and size.

4. Click **OK**.

Delete formatting and items

As your notebook evolves, you will probably want to remove formatting from some of your items, or perhaps delete the items entirely. Clearing all formatting from an item leaves the text in place but removes formatting such as bold, italics, and highlighting. If you changed the font used to display your text, when you remove the formatting, OneNote also changes the item's font back to Calibri. Deleting an item is a straightforward operation you can accomplish by using the ribbon or your keyboard.

 SEE ALSO For more information about cutting a note or part of a note so it is available to paste from the Clipboard, see "Create, cut, and copy notes" earlier in this chapter.

To clear formatting from a note

1. Do either of the following:

   - Click anywhere in the paragraph from which you want to remove formatting.

   - Select the paragraphs from which you want to remove formatting.

2. Do either of the following:

   - On the **Home** tab of the ribbon, in the **Basic Text** group, click the **Clear All Formatting** button.

   - Press **Ctrl+Shift+N**.

To delete an item

1. Click the title bar of the item.

2. On the **Home** tab of the ribbon, in the **Basic Text** group, click the **Delete** button.

Skills review

In this chapter, you learned how to:

2

- Create, cut, and copy notes

- Apply text formatting to notes

- Create lists and outlines

- Change paragraph formatting

- Delete formatting and items

Practice tasks

The practice files for these tasks are located in the OneNoteSBS\Ch02 folder. The results of the tasks will be automatically saved into the same file in the same folder.

Create, cut, and copy notes

Open the CreateNotes section in OneNote, and then perform the following tasks:

1. Add a new note to the page; the new note should contain a due date for the project plan to be submitted.

2. Select and delete the existing text that reminds you to find out the due date for the project plan.

3. Copy the text from the separate item that tells you to verify how delivery affects the next steps of the project, and paste it into the note you created in step 1.

Apply text formatting to notes

Open the FormatNotes section in OneNote, and then perform the following tasks:

1. Apply the **Heading 1** style to the first line of text in the note.

2. Apply bold and red font color formatting to the word *Important*.

3. Apply italic formatting to the word *statistical*.

4. Highlight the words *by the end of the week* by using the highlight color of your choice.

Create lists and outlines

Open the CreateLists section in OneNote, and then perform the following tasks:

1. Format the list on the left side of the page as a numbered list.

2. Format the list on the right side of the page as a bulleted list.

3. In the numbered list, move the items marked **6** and **7** to the second level of the numbered list by indenting their lines.

4. Change the style of bullets used for the bulleted list.

5. By dragging its item indicator, move the *Test with water and target liquid* item from the bulleted list to the bottom of the numbered list.

Change paragraph formatting

Open the FormatParagraphs section in OneNote, and then perform the following tasks:

1. Center the header at the top of the note.

2. Reposition the indented item so it is in line with the items around it.

3. Select the *Process Steps* header and apply paragraph formatting so there are 10 points of white space after the text.

4. Select the remaining lines in the note and apply paragraph formatting so each line takes up at least 18 points of space.

Delete formatting and items

Open the DeleteFormatting section in OneNote, and then perform the following tasks:

1. Clear all formatting from all the items on the left side of the page.

2. Delete the item titled **Ideas** on the right side of the page.

Work with your notes

3

Many of the notes you make in your OneNote notebooks will consist of text that you type or write onto a page. If you want to make a quick note without opening OneNote, you can do so by using tools on the Windows taskbar. After you create the quick note, you can add it to your notebook. You can also organize your data by using tables, attach files and printouts, and add images to help make your notes clear.

If you want to create a clickable link to an outside source, such as a webpage, file, or location within a OneNote notebook, you can do so. You can also add media content by recording an audio or video note, identify when you made a note by adding a time and date stamp, and capture mathematical information by using symbols and equations.

This chapter guides you through procedures related to creating quick notes, adding tables, attaching files and printouts, adding images and screen clippings, creating links to resources, recording audio and video notes, inserting time and date stamps, and adding symbols and equations.

In this chapter

- Create quick notes
- Add tables
- Attach files and printouts
- Add images and screen clippings
- Create links to resources
- Record audio and video notes
- Insert time and date stamps
- Add symbols and equations

Practice files

For this chapter, use the practice files from the OneNoteSBS\Ch03 folder. For practice file download instructions, see the introduction.

Create quick notes

Great ideas come from articles you read, videos you watch, and associations you make when you're doing other work. You can capture those ideas in OneNote by creating a quick note. Installing OneNote adds the OneNote icon (an icon of the letter *N* with a pair of scissors) to the hidden icons tray on the Windows taskbar. The default behavior of this icon is to create a quick note when it is clicked.

Use the OneNote icon to create a quick note

When you create a new quick note, OneNote opens a small window where you can enter your note and format its text.

 TIP You can change the behavior of the icon in the tray on the Windows taskbar so that clicking it takes a screen clipping or opens the full OneNote app.

After you create a quick note from Windows, you can view it within your OneNote notebook, copy it to a new location in OneNote, or get rid of it entirely. You can also use the OneNote icon's options to capture a screen clipping, which is an image of a portion of your computer display.

 SEE ALSO For more information about working with screen clippings, see "Add images and screen clippings" later in this chapter.

To create a quick note

1. Do either of the following:

   - On the Windows taskbar, click the **Show hidden icons** arrow, and then click the **OneNote** icon.

   - Press **Windows logo key+N**.

2. In the quick note window, type or write the note's text.

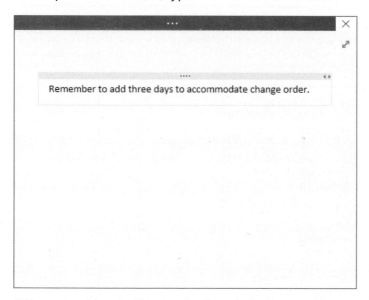

Add text to a quick note without starting the main OneNote app

3. Click the **Close** button in the upper-right corner of the quick note window to close the window.

To format a quick note

1. Click the **Auto-Hide Ribbon** button (the three dots) at the center of the quick note window's title bar to display the ribbon.

2. Use the buttons on the ribbon tabs to format your quick note's contents.

To open a quick note in its OneNote page

1. Click the **Normal View** button (the two-headed arrow) in the upper-right corner of the quick note.

2. Browse your OneNote notebooks and tabs to see where your Quick Notes tab is.

3. Right-click the page name, **Untitled page**, click **Rename**, type a new name for the page, and press **Enter**.

> ✅ **TIP** If you have OneNote open, this might open a second instance. When your quick note appears as a page in OneNote, you'll know it's a quick note because it has a pink or salmon-colored background (instead of white), and it won't have the page title section at the top like the other OneNote pages.

To change the default quick note operation

1. On the Windows taskbar, click the **Show hidden icons** button, right-click the **OneNote** icon, point to **OneNote icon defaults**, and click one of these options:

   - **New quick note**
   - **Open OneNote**
   - **Take screen clipping**

To turn off quick notes

1. On the Windows taskbar, click the **Show hidden icons** button, right-click the **OneNote** icon, and then click **Close**.

To view a quick note within a notebook

1. Open a notebook.

2. Click the **Click to view other notebooks** button in the upper-left corner of the screen (the button displays the name of your notebook and a downward-pointing arrow).

3. At the bottom of the list, click **Quick Notes**.

Add tables

One of the strengths of OneNote is that you can use it to type or write notes anywhere on a page, creating layouts that capture the information you want to retain and displaying the notes in a way that helps you process what you learned. Some data, however, is more suited to a table, with well-defined rows and columns.

Package Tracking

Friday, November 6, 2015   11:12 PM

Category	Volume
Ground	305,902
3Day	171,547
2Day	143,861
Overnight	34,003

Use tables to organize numerical data

When you create a table, you specify the number of rows and columns it will contain. After your table is in place, you can add or remove rows or columns, change the height of a row or the width of a column, and select columns or rows so you can format or delete their contents in one action.

 TIP One common way to format table column headers (the top row) is to align their text with the center of the column and add bold formatting.

You can change the appearance of your table's text by selecting the cells you want to format and applying the formatting you want. If you want to affect the table as a whole, such as by showing or hiding cell borders or adding a background color to selected table cells, you can do so quickly. You can also format the position of text within a cell, aligning the text with the left edge, center, or right edge of a cell.

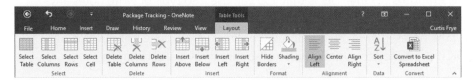

Use the Table Tools Layout tool tab to edit and format your table

If you record business data in a notebook, such as monthly sales for various departments, you might find it useful to sort the data based on the contents of a column. You can sort from the largest value to the smallest, or smallest to largest, as your analysis requires. To focus on a subset of your data, you can also sort a subset of the rows in your table.

To create a table

1. Click on the page where you want to insert the table.

2. On the **Insert** tab of the ribbon, in the **Tables** group, click **Table**, and then click the box that represents the number of columns and rows you want in your table.

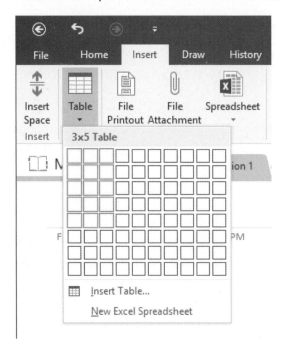

Select the number of rows and columns to include in your table

Or

1. Click on the page where you want to insert the table.

2. On the **Insert** tab, in the **Tables** group, click **Table**, and then click **Insert Table**.

3. In the **Insert Table** dialog box, in the **Number of columns** box, enter the number of columns you want in your table.

4. In the **Number of rows** box, enter the number of rows you want in your table.

5. Click **OK**.

To enter or edit the contents of a table cell

1. Click in the cell where you want to enter or edit content.

2. Use data entry, editing, and formatting techniques, such as typing, pasting, and inserting attachments or images, to change the content of the cell.

To move within a table

1. Use any of the following techniques to move within a table:

   - Press **Tab** to move one cell to the right.

     > ✓ **TIP** Pressing Tab when you are in the last cell in a row selects the cell at the start of the row below the active row. If you are in the last cell of the table, pressing Tab creates a new row.

   - Press **Shift+Tab** to move one cell to the left. (The cursor stops when you reach the first cell.)

   - Press an arrow key to move in the direction of the arrow (left, right, up, or down), as follows:

     - Press the **Right Arrow** key when the cursor is in the last cell in a row to select the cell at the start of the row below the active row.

     - If there is a line of text already below the table, press the **Right Arrow** key in the last cell of the table to move below the table. (If the table is at the bottom of the active note, the cursor stops in the last cell of the table.)

     - In any cell in the bottom row of the table, press the **Down Arrow** key to move below the table. (If the table is at the bottom of the note, this action creates a new line.)

- Press the **Left Arrow** key when the cursor is in the first cell in a row to select the cell at the end of the row above the active row.

- If the cursor is in the first cell of the table, press the **Left Arrow** or **Up Arrow** key to move to the line above the table.

To select a table cell

1. Click in the cell you want to select.

2. Do either of the following:

   - On the **Layout** tool tab, in the **Select** group, click **Select Cell**.

   - Press **Ctrl+A** twice.

> 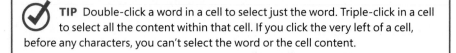 **TIP** Double-click a word in a cell to select just the word. Triple-click in a cell to select all the content within that cell. If you click the very left of a cell, before any characters, you can't select the word or the cell content.

Or

1. Right-click in the cell you want to select, point to **Table**, and then click **Select Cell**.

To select multiple table cells

1. Click within the first table cell you want to select, and then drag the pointer to select the cells.

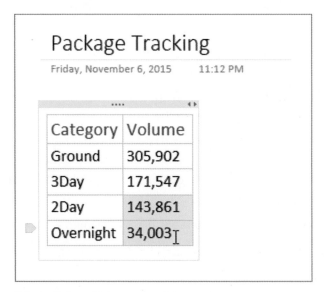

Select cells in multiple rows or columns

To select the entire table

1. Click any cell in the table.

2. Do either of the following:

   - On the **Layout** tool tab, in the **Select** group, click **Select Table**.

   - Press **Ctrl+A** four times.

Or

1. Right-click any cell in the table, point to **Table**, and then click **Select Table**.

To select a table column

1. Click any cell in the column you want to select.

2. On the **Layout** tool tab, in the **Select** group, click **Select Columns**.

Or

1. Point to the area just above the top of the column you want to select.

2. After your cursor changes to a black downward-pointing arrow, click the column.

Or

1. Right-click any cell in the column you want to select. Point to **Table**, and then click **Select Columns**.

To select multiple table columns

1. Select cells in the columns you want to select.

2. Do either of the following:

   - On the **Layout** tool tab, click **Select Columns**.

   - Right-click the selected cells, point to **Table**, and then click **Select Columns**.

To select a table row

1. Click any cell in the row you want to select.

2. Do either of the following:

   - On the **Layout** tool tab, in the **Select** group, click **Select Rows**.

   - Press **Ctrl+A** three times.

Or

1. Point to the row you want to select.

2. Click the item indicator to the left of the row.

Or

1. Right-click any cell in the row you want to select. Point to **Table**, and then click **Select Rows**.

To select multiple table rows

1. Select cells in the rows you want to select.

2. Do either of the following:

   - On the **Layout** tool tab, click **Select Rows**.

   - Right-click the selected cells, point to **Table**, and then click **Select Rows**.

To insert a table row

1. Click a cell in the row above or below where you want to insert the row.

2. On the **Layout** tool tab, in the **Insert** group, do either of the following:

   - Click **Insert Above** to insert a row above the row that contains the active cell.

   - Click **Insert Below** to insert a row below the row that contains the active cell.

Or

1. Right-click a cell in the row above or below where you want to insert the row.

2. Point to **Table**, and do either of the following:

   - Click **Insert Above** to insert a row above the row that contains the active cell.

   - Click **Insert Below** to insert a row below the row that contains the active cell.

To insert multiple table rows

1. Above or below where you want to insert the rows, select cells in the same number of rows as the rows you want to insert.

2. On the **Layout** tool tab, in the **Insert** group, do either of the following:

   - Click **Insert Above** to insert the rows above the selected cells' rows.

   - Click **Insert Below** to insert the rows below the selected cells' rows.

Or

1. Above or below where you want to insert the rows, select cells in the same number of rows as the rows you want to insert.

2. Right-click the selected cells, point to **Table**, and do either of the following:

   - Click **Insert Above** to insert rows above the rows that contain the active cells.

   - Click **Insert Below** to insert rows below the rows that contain the active cells.

3

To insert a table column

1. Click a cell in the column to the left or right of where you want to insert the new column.

2. On the **Layout** tool tab, in the **Insert** group, do either of the following:

   - Click **Insert Left** to insert a column to the left of the column that contains the active cell.

   - Click **Insert Right** to insert a column to the right of the column that contains the active cell.

Or

1. Right-click a cell in the column to the left or right of where you want to insert the new column.

2. Point to **Table**, and do either of the following:

   - Click **Insert Left** to insert a column to the left of the column that contains the active cell.

   - Click **Insert Right** to insert a column to the right of the column that contains the active cell.

To insert multiple table columns

1. To the left or right of where you want to insert the columns, select cells in the same number of columns as the columns you want to insert.

2. On the **Layout** tool tab, in the **Insert** group, do either of the following:

   - Click **Insert Left** to insert the columns to the left of the selected columns.

   - Click **Insert Right** to insert the columns to the right of the selected columns.

Or

1. To the left or right of where you want to insert the columns, select cells in the same number of columns as the columns you want to insert.

2. Right-click the selected cells, point to **Table**, and do either of the following:

   - Click **Insert Left** to insert the columns to the left of the columns that contain the active cells.

   - Click **Insert Right** to insert the columns to the right of the columns that contain the active cells.

To hide or show table borders

1. Click any cell in the table.

2. On the **Layout** tool tab, in the **Format** group, click **Hide Borders**.

Or

1. Right-click any cell in the table, point to **Table**, and then click **Hide Borders**.

To change the background color of table cells

1. Select the cells to which you want to apply the formatting.

2. Do either of the following:

   - On the **Layout** tool tab, in the **Format** group, click **Shading**.

   - Right-click the selected cells, point to **Table**, and then point to **Shading**.

3. Do either of the following:

   - In the palette that appears, click the color you want to apply.

   - Click **More Colors** to open the Colors dialog box. Select a new color, and then click **OK**.

3

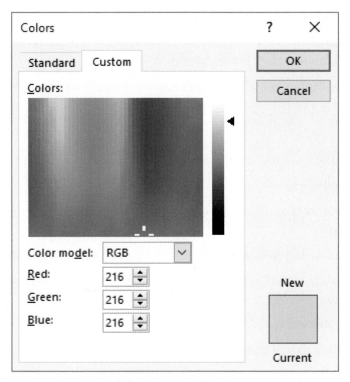

Select precise colors by using the Colors dialog box

To change the alignment of a table cell's contents

1. Select the table cells you want to format.

2. On the **Layout** tool tab, in the **Alignment** group, click an alignment option (**Align Left**, **Center**, or **Align Right**), to apply it to the selected cells.

To sort data based on a table column's values

1. Click any cell in the column you want to sort.

2. Do either of the following:

   • On the **Layout** tool tab, in the **Data** group, click **Sort**.

   • Right-click the cell, and point to **Table**.

3. Do either of the following:

- Click **Sort Ascending** to sort the table's rows in ascending order (smallest to largest) based on the values in the column.

- Click **Sort Descending** to sort the table's rows in descending order (largest to smallest) based on the values in the column.

To sort selected values only

1. Select the cells in the rows you want to sort.

2. Do either of the following:

- On the **Layout** tool tab, in the **Data** group, click **Sort**, and then click **Sort Selected Rows**.

- Right-click the selected cells, point to **Table**, and then click **Sort Selected Rows**.

3. In the **Sort** dialog box, in the **Sort by** list, click the name of the column by which you want to sort the selected rows.

4. Do either of the following:

- Select **Ascending** to sort the rows in ascending order.

- Select **Descending** to sort the rows in descending order.

5. Click **OK**.

To delete a table

1. Click in any cell in the table.

2. Do either of the following:

- On the **Layout** tool tab, in the **Delete** group, click **Delete Table**.

- Press **Ctrl+A** four times.

3. Press **Delete**.

Or

1. Right-click anywhere in the table, point to **Table**, and then click **Delete Table**.

Attach files and printouts

OneNote works well with other Microsoft Office apps. One of the ways you can work with other files is to include them as printouts or attachments. In OneNote, a printout displays the contents of another file in its entirety. If you have a one-page description of service levels saved as a Microsoft Word document, for example, you can display the document as a printout on a OneNote page.

3

Include a file as a printout to see its full contents in OneNote

> ⚠ **IMPORTANT** When you insert a file as a printout, the entire file appears on the page. Word files appear as multiple images in OneNote, where each page of the document gets its own image on the page.

After you add a printout to your notebook, you can change its label, refresh the print-out if you believe the source file has changed, or even save the file under a new name on your computer. If you want to work with a file that has been included as a printout, you can open the file in its original program, if you have the program installed on your computer. When you no longer need the printout in your notebook, you can delete it.

Attaching a file creates a link to the file but doesn't include its contents in your notebook like adding a printout does. Instead, you can double-click the icon that represents the attached file to view or edit it in its source program. You can, if you want, convert the attached file to a printout. If you no longer need a reference to the attached file, you can delete it.

To include a printout in a notebook

1. Click the page after which you want to insert the printout.

> **TIP** The printout might be multiple pages, depending on the length of the original file. The first page starts immediately after your current page and is given the name of the original file. Subsequent pages are named Page 2, Page 3, and so on, and are indented one level below the first page.

2. On the **Insert** tab of the ribbon, in the **Files** group, click **File Printout**.

3. In the **Choose Document to Insert** dialog box, click the file you want to include as a printout, and then click **Insert**.

To open the original printout source file in its native program

1. At the top of the first printout page, right-click the icon that represents the file you want to open, and then click **Open Original**.

To change the printout label in OneNote

1. Right-click the icon that represents the printout, and then click **Rename**.

2. In the **Rename** dialog box, enter a new name for the file label.

3. Click **OK**.

To save the included printout file under a new name

1. Right-click the icon that represents the printout, and then click **Save As**.

2. In the **Save As** dialog box, navigate to the folder where you want to save a copy of the file.

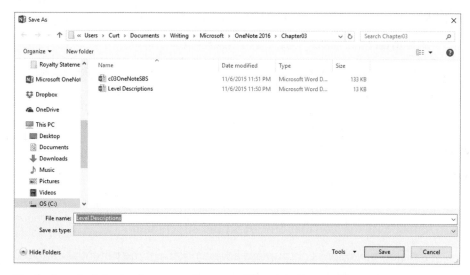

Use the Save As dialog box to save another copy of the printout source file

3. In the **File name** box, enter a new name for the file.

4. Click **Save**.

To refresh the printout from the original file

1. Right-click the icon representing the printout, and then click **Refresh Printout**.

2. If a dialog box opens and displays a warning about the potential dangers of opening unknown files, click **OK** to refresh the printout.

To delete a printout

1. Right-click the header that represents the printout, and then click **Remove Printout**.

To attach a file to a notebook page

1. Click the page where you want to insert the file icon.

2. On the **Insert** tab, in the **Files** group, click **File Attachment**.

3. In the **Choose a file or set of files to insert** dialog box, browse to and select the file or files you want to attach to the page, and then click **Insert**.

4. In the **Insert File** dialog box, click **Attach File**.

5. In the text area below the attachment's icon, enter text to describe the attached file.

Or

1. From File Explorer, drag the file onto the OneNote page and drop it where you want to insert the file icon.

2. In the **Insert File** dialog box, click **Attach File**.

To open an attached file

1. Double-click the icon that represents the attachment.

2. If a dialog box opens and displays a warning about the potential dangers of opening unknown files, click **OK** to open the file.

> IMPORTANT To open the attached file, you must have the source program installed, such as Microsoft Word or Excel.

To convert an attached file to a printout

1. Right-click the icon that represents the attachment, and then click **Insert as Printout**.

To delete an attachment

1. Click the attachment to select it.

2. Press **Delete**.

Add images and screen clippings

Most of the notes you add to your OneNote notebooks will probably be in the form of written and typed text. That said, there are many occasions when the appropriate image provides much more information than a few sentences could. Whether you insert an image related to a product prototype or capture an image of part of your screen to share software instructions with your team, images add substantial value to your notes.

3

You can add images from a variety of sources, including your computer, your OneDrive account, or Bing Image Search. You can use Bing Image Search to search online for images that are licensed under a Creative Commons license, but you should be sure that the conditions applied to a specific image, such as no commercial use, permit you to use the image in your notebook.

> ⚠ **IMPORTANT** If you aren't sure whether an image's licensing terms permit your usage, consult with an intellectual property attorney. If any doubt remains, it's safest to use an image with licensing terms that clearly allow for your planned use.

Another method for adding an image to a notebook is to capture part of your screen as a screen clipping, which you can then add to your notebook.

When your image is part of your notebook, you can move it, resize it, make it the page's background image, add alternative text for screen readers or web browsers, and save the image as a separate file for use in other programs. If your image contains text, you can have OneNote copy text from the image so you can use it elsewhere, and you can make the image's text searchable.

> **TIP** OneNote's text recognition routines are good, but not completely accurate. It's likely you will need to edit the text after it's been extracted.

To insert an image from your computer

1. Click the page where you want to insert the image.

2. On the **Insert** tab, in the **Images** group, click **Pictures**.

3. In the **Insert Picture** dialog box, navigate to the folder that contains the image you want to add.

4. Click the image, and then click **Open**.

Insert images to add information and appeal to your notebook

To insert an image from OneDrive

1. Click the page where you want to insert the image.

2. On the **Insert** tab, in the **Images** group, click **Online Pictures**.

3. In the **Insert Pictures** dialog box, click **OneDrive – Personal**.

> **TIP** You might not see a OneDrive - Personal option. To connect to your OneDrive account and to see the OneDrive option, click the Sign In With Your Microsoft Account link at the bottom of the Insert Pictures dialog box.

4. Navigate to the folder that contains the image you want to add.

5. Click the image, and then click **Insert**.

To insert an image from Bing Image Search

1. Click the page where you want to insert the image.

2. On the **Insert** tab, in the **Images** group, click **Online Pictures**.

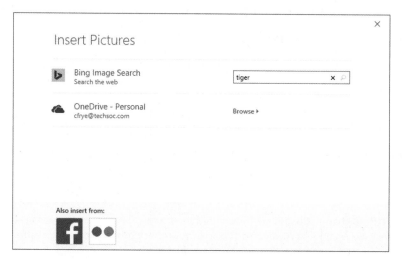

Find pictures online by using Bing Image Search

3. In the **Insert Pictures** dialog box, enter a search term in the text box and press **Enter**.

4. Read the message about image licenses and rights.

5. In the gallery of images, click the image you want to add, and then click **Insert**.

> ✓ **TIP** You can also insert images from Facebook and Flickr. To sign in to those services and access the images, in the Also Insert From section at the bottom of the Insert Pictures dialog box, click the Facebook or Flickr icon and follow the appropriate sign-in procedure.

To capture a screen clipping

1. Do either of the following:

    - On the Windows taskbar, click the **Show hidden icons** button, right-click the **OneNote** icon, and then click **Take screen clipping**.

    - Press **Windows logo key+Shift+S**.

2. Click and drag over the area to select the part of the screen you want to capture as an image.

3. In the **Select Location in OneNote** dialog box, do either of the following:

    - Use the tools in the **All Notebooks** pane to select the location in which you want to place the clipping, and then click **Send to Selected Location**.

    - Click **Copy to Clipboard** to copy the image to the Clipboard.

> ✅ **TIP** To change the default behavior of the Screen Clipping tool, select the Don't Ask Me Again And Always Do The Following check box, and then click either Send To Selected Location or Copy To Clipboard.

Or

1. Click the page where you want to insert the screen clipping.

2. On the **Insert** tab, in the **Images** group, click **Screen Clipping**.

3. Drag to select the part of the screen you want to capture. When you release the left mouse button, an image of the selected area of the screen appears in your notebook.

To rotate an image

1. Right-click the image, point to **Rotate**, and then click the option that describes how you want to rotate or flip the image.

To move an image

1. Point to the image.

2. When the pointer changes to a four-headed arrow, drag the image to a new location.

 TIP If you're having trouble selecting an image, right-click the image, and then click Move. Reposition the image, and then click away from it to release the selection.

3

To resize an image

1. Click the image to select it.

2. Drag any of the handles on the corners or sides of the image to change the image's size.

To restore an image to its original size

1. Right-click the image, and then click **Restore to Original Size**.

To save an image as a separate file

1. Right-click the image, and then click **Save As**.

2. In the **Save As** dialog box, navigate to the folder where you want to save the image.

3. In the **File name** box, enter a name for the new file.

4. Click **Save**.

To set an image as a page's background

1. Right-click the image, and then click **Set Picture as Background**.

To copy text from an image

1. Right-click the image that contains the text you want to copy, and then click **Copy Text from Picture**.

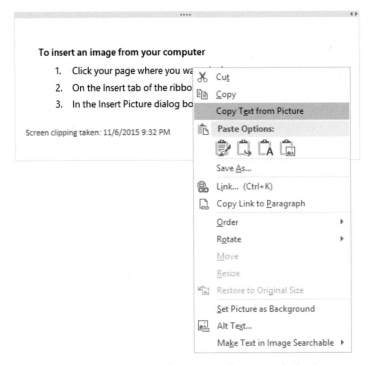

Use text recognition to copy text from screen clippings and other images

2. Paste the copied text elsewhere in your notebook or in another document.

> **TIP** Copying text from an image can be helpful if all you have is a copy of an image, but what you really want is the text so that you can format or edit it. For example, if you have a video recording of a Skype online meeting in which the presenter uses a Microsoft PowerPoint deck, you could capture screenshots of the slides in the deck and paste them into OneNote by using the screen clipping capture technique described in this topic. With the screen clipping images in place, you can paste the copied text onto the page and format it as a note.

To make text within an image searchable

1. Right-click the image that contains the text you want to copy, point to **Make Text in Image Searchable**, and then click the language of the text. (Only English, French, and Spanish are currently available.)

To remove image text from the notebook's collection of searchable text

1. Right-click the image that contains the text you want to remove from the collection, point to **Make Text in Image Searchable**, and then click **Disabled**.

Create links to resources

The Office apps work well together and provide terrific access to web-based resources via links. You can use links (*link* is short for *hyperlink*) to create clickable text, images, and shapes that lead users to the webpages, files, or OneNote notebook locations you identify. If needed, you can find the link address of an object in your notebook.

3

Define a link to a resource by using the Link dialog box

Following a link just requires the reader to click the link within the notebook. After the resource appears, the reader can move back to the notebook page from which he or she started or move forward to the linked resource. Editing a link lets you change its characteristics (such as the object pointed to by the link), whereas deleting a link removes the connectivity but leaves the text or object you used as a base.

To create a link to a web resource

1. Do one of the following:

   - Click the page where you want to insert the link.

   - Select the text to be formatted as a hyperlink.

   - Select the item to serve as the anchor for the hyperlink.

2. Do either of the following to open the Link dialog box:

   - On the **Insert** tab of the ribbon, in the **Links** group, click **Link**.

   - Press **Ctrl+K**.

3. In the **Link** dialog box, edit the contents of the **Text to display** box to specify the text that will serve as the hyperlink.

4. Do either of the following:

   - In the **Address** box, enter the address of the webpage to which you want to link.

   - Click the **Browse the Web** button to open your default web browser, navigate to the webpage to which you want to link, copy the page's address, and paste it into the **Address** box.

5. Click **OK**.

To create a link to a file

1. Do one of the following:

   - Click the page where you want to insert the link.

   - Select the text to be formatted as a hyperlink.

   - Select the item to serve as the anchor for the hyperlink.

2. Do either of the following:

   - On the **Insert** tab, in the **Links** group, click **Link**.

   - Press **Ctrl+K**.

3. In the **Link** dialog box, edit the contents of the **Text to display** box to specify the text that will serve as the hyperlink.

4. Click the **Browse for File** button.

5. In the **Link to File** dialog box, click the file to which you want to link, and then click **Open**.

6. Click **OK**.

To create a link to a location in OneNote

1. Do one of the following:

   - Click the page where you want to insert the link.

   - Select the text to be formatted as a hyperlink.

   - Select the item to serve as the anchor for the hyperlink.

2. Do either of the following:

   - On the **Insert** tab, in the **Links** group, click **Link**.

   - Press **Ctrl+K**.

3. In the **Link** dialog box, edit the contents of the **Text to display** box to specify the text that will serve as the hyperlink.

4. Use the tools available in the **Or pick a location in OneNote** pane to identify the location to which you want to link.

5. Click **OK**.

To copy the link address of a OneNote object

1. Right-click the item to which you want to create a link (such as text, a table cell, or an image), and then click **Copy Link to Paragraph**.

2. Do one of the following:

   - Click the page where you want to insert the link.

   - Select the text to be formatted as a hyperlink.

   - Select the item to serve as the anchor for the hyperlink.

3. Do either of the following:

   - On the **Insert** tab, in the **Links** group, click **Link**.

   - Press **Ctrl+K**.

4. In the **Link** dialog box, paste the copied link address into the **Address** box.

5. Click **OK**.

To follow a link

1. Click the item or text identified as a hyperlink.

To go back after following a link

1. On the **Quick Access Toolbar**, click the **Back** button.

Click the Back or Forward button to move between resources

To go forward to a previously followed link

1. On the **Quick Access Toolbar**, click the **Forward** button.

To edit a link

1. Do either of the following:

    -   Select the linked text, and on the **Insert** tab, in the **Links** group, click **Link**.

    -   Right-click the link you want to edit, and then click **Edit Link**.

2. Use the tools in the **Link** dialog box to edit the hyperlink.

3. Click **OK**.

To copy a link

1. Do either of the following:

    -   Right-click the link and then click **Copy Link** to copy just the link address.

    -   Select the hyperlinked text, and press **Ctrl+C**.

 TIP You can copy the link address, but it might be faster and more useful to copy and reuse the hyperlinked text.

To remove a link

1. Right-click the link, and then click **Remove Link**.

    This removes the hyperlink but keeps the underlying text or object.

Record audio and video notes

Contemporary computers are powerful enough to handle audio and video files easily, so it makes sense that you would be able to capture audio and video notes in OneNote. Before you record an audio or video note, you should make sure to identify the devices to use for those tasks and set the format for your recording. Choosing a higher resolution improves the audio or video quality of your recording, at the expense of taking up more room on your hard drive.

After you record an audio or video note, you can play it back in OneNote. The controls you use will be familiar if you've watched video online or by using a DVD player.

Control audio and video playback by using these buttons

Finally, you can change the text associated with a recording, or delete the recording if you no longer need it.

To select an audio input device

1. Click the **File** tab to open the Backstage view, and then click **Options**.

2. In the **OneNote Options** dialog box, click **Audio & Video** in the navigation pane on the left.

3. On the **Audio & Video** page, in the **Audio recording settings** area, in the **Device** list, click the device to use for audio input.

4. If necessary, in the **Input** list, click the input setting you want to use.

5. If necessary, in the **Codec** list, click the encoding scheme you want to use.

6. If necessary, in the **Format** list, click the format you want to use.

>  **TIP** The default audio settings will work under most circumstances, but you can change them if your information technology department recommends another configuration.

7. Click **OK**.

To select a video input device

1. In the **OneNote Options** dialog box, click **Audio & Video**.

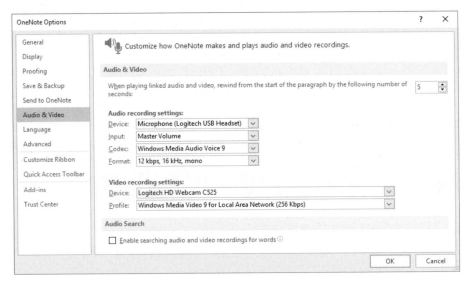

Set your audio and video options by using tools in the OneNote Options dialog box

2. On the **Audio & Video** page, in the **Video recording settings** area, in the **Device** list, click the device to use for video input.

3. If necessary, in the **Profile** list, click the encoding scheme you want to use.

> **TIP** The default video settings will work under most circumstances, but you can change them if your information technology department recommends another configuration.

4. Click **OK**.

To record an audio note

1. On a notebook page, click where you want to insert the icon for the audio note.

2. On the **Insert** tab, in the **Recording** group, click **Record Audio**.

3. Record your audio note.

4. On the **Playback** tool tab, in the **Playback** group, click **Stop**.

To record a video note

1. On a notebook page, click where you want to insert the icon for the video note.

2. On the **Insert** tab, in the **Recording** group, click **Record Video**.

3. Record your video note.

4. On the **Playback** tool tab, in the **Playback** group, click **Stop**.

> **TIP** While recording an audio or video note, you can take notes (typed or written with a stylus) and insert images or objects. After you click Stop to end the recording, small Play buttons appear to the left of each note. You can click each play button to jump to the time of the recording when that note was taken and understand the note in context.

To play an audio or video note

1. Click the icon representing the audio or video note.

2. In the control bar that appears, click the **Play** button.

    Or

    On the **Playback** tool tab, in the **Playback** group, click the **Play** button.

3. Use the remaining controls on the **Playback** tool tab to pause, rewind, and fast-forward the note.

To rename an audio or video note

1. Right-click the icon representing the note, and then click **Rename**.

2. In the **Rename File** dialog box, enter a new name for the note.

3. Click **OK**.

To delete an audio or video note

1. Right-click the icon representing the note, and then click **Cut**.

Or

1. Click the audio or video note to select it.

2. Press the **Delete** key.

Insert time and date stamps

In many cases, when something happens is as important as what happens. For example, you might want to note the exact time a colleague brought up an idea in a meeting, or record the time and date when you finished working on a proposal.

In OneNote, you can add the current time, the current date, or both the current date and time to your notebook. Unless you edit their text, these values don't change when you close and reopen your notebook, so you have a record of when you added the time or date stamp.

To insert only the current date

1. On a notebook page, click where you want to insert the date.

2. Do either of the following:

   - On the **Insert** tab of the ribbon, in the **Time Stamp** group, click **Date**.

   - Press **Alt+Shift+D**. (D is for date.)

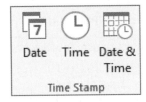

Add Date, Time, or Date & Time stamps to your notebook

To insert only the current time

1. Click where you want to insert the time.

2. Do either of the following:

   - On the **Insert** tab, in the **Time Stamp** group, click **Time**.

   - Press **Alt+Shift+T**. (T is for time.)

To insert the current date and time

1. Click where you want to insert the date and time.

2. On the **Insert** tab, in the **Time Stamp** group, click **Date & Time**.

Add symbols and equations

Much of the work you do in OneNote will use standard letters and numbers. If you work in a legal or technical field, though, you might use special characters such as the copyright or trademark symbols in your work. In OneNote, you can quickly add any of a set of frequently used symbols.

3

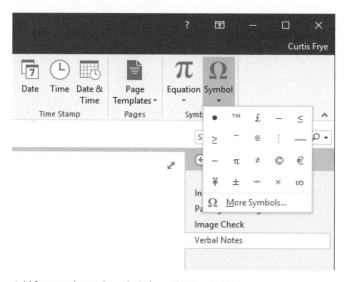

Add frequently used symbols from the Symbol list

If the gallery of frequently used symbols doesn't contain the symbol you want to add, you might be able to find it in the character set of a font installed on your system. You can look through your fonts to find the character you want. OneNote and other Office apps divide each font into subsets of characters, such as mathematical symbols, Cyrillic alphabet characters, and Roman alphabet characters, to make searching for the character you want easier.

 IMPORTANT If you do locate the symbol you want, be sure to write down its Unicode or ASCII character code and the font name so you can find it again.

For mathematical applications, such as statistical analysis or calculus, you can represent equations on a page by using mathematical notation.

OneNote has a gallery of pre-built equations, such as the Pythagorean Theorem and the quadratic formula, that you can add from the ribbon.

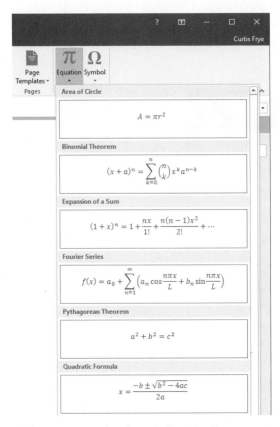

Add common equations from the Equation list

You can also build equations from a series of frameworks, which you can find on the Equation Tools Design tool tab that appears when you select an equation.

You can change the way OneNote displays the equation or edit the equation's contents. Editing an equation is a matter of clicking within the body of the equation to activate it, and then editing its contents to create exactly the equation you want. If you decide you no longer need an equation, you can always delete it.

> **TIP** If the equation's text boxes are too small for you to edit its contents effectively, select the equation and increase its font size until you can work with the text easily. After you finish editing your equation, you can select it again and reduce the font size for sharing and publication.

To add a frequently used symbol

1. Position the cursor at the location where you want to add the symbol.

2. On the **Insert** tab of the ribbon, in the **Symbols** group, click **Symbol**.

3. In the gallery that appears, click the symbol you want to add to your page.

To add a character from any available font

1. Position the cursor at the location where you want to add the symbol.

2. On the **Insert** tab, click **Symbol**.

3. In the gallery that appears, click **More Symbols**.

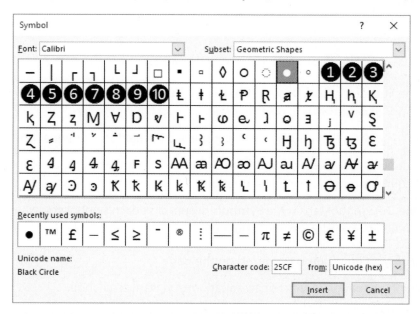

Select a symbol to insert into a notebook by using the Symbol dialog box

4. In the **Symbol** dialog box, click the **Font** list arrow, and then click the font from which you want to select the symbol.

5. Click the **Subset** list arrow, and then click the subset from which you want to select the symbol.

6. Click the symbol you want to include.

7. Click **Insert**.

8. When you are finished inserting symbols, click **Close**.

To add a common equation

1. Position the cursor at the location where you want to add the equation.

2. On the **Insert** tab, in the **Symbols** group, click the **Equation** list arrow, and then click the equation you want to add.

To create a custom equation

1. Position the cursor at the location where you want to add the equation.

2. On the **Insert** tab, in the **Symbols** group, click **Equation**.

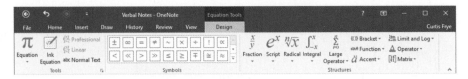

Use the tools on the Equation Tools Design tool tab to create a custom equation

3. On the **Equation Tools Design** tool tab, in the **Structures** group, click the category of equation you want to create.

4. From the gallery that appears, click the specific format for your equation.

5. In your note, click in each editable area of the equation form and enter the text and numbers required for your equation.

6. On the **Design** tool tab, in the **Symbols** group, click each symbol you want to add in the proper place in your equation.

To change how an equation is rendered on the page

1. Select the equation (or part of an equation) you want to change.

2. On the **Design** tool tab, in the **Tools** group, do one of the following:

   - Click **Professional** to display the equation in two-dimensional format (characters stacked vertically) by using mathematics-specific text.

   - Click **Linear** to display the equation in one-dimensional format by using mathematics-specific text.

 TIP You can also access the Professional and Linear options by right-clicking your selected equation and clicking Professional or Linear.

- Click **Normal Text** to use non-mathematical text in the part of the page that contains an equation.

> ✓ **TIP** Normal Text changes your mathematical formatting to standard text formatting. You keep the two-dimensional stacking, but you lose the spacing and italicized font style that you expect to see in mathematical instructions. This can be useful when you are referring to an equation in a paragraph.

3

To edit an equation

1. Click within the body of the equation to activate it.

2. Position the cursor where you want to make your change, and use the keyboard and commands on the ribbon to edit the equation.

To delete an equation

1. Select the equation text that you want to delete, or select the item that contains the equation.

2. Do one of the following:

   - Press **Delete**.

   - On the **Home** tab, in the **Basic Text** group, click **Delete**.

   - Right-click the selection, and click **Cut**.

Skills review

In this chapter, you learned how to:

- Create quick notes

- Add tables

- Attach files and printouts

- Add images and screen clippings

- Create links to resources

- Record audio and video notes

- Insert time and date stamps

- Add symbols and equations

Practice tasks

The practice files for these tasks are located in the OneNoteSBS\Ch03 folder. The results of the tasks will be automatically saved into the same file in the same folder.

Create quick notes

In Windows, perform the following tasks:

1. Open any notebook in OneNote, and then use the tools on the Windows taskbar to create a quick note on the active notebook page.

2. In the quick note window, display the ribbon and add formatting to the note you created.

3. Open the quick note you just created in the OneNote app.

Add tables

Open the AddTables section in OneNote, and then perform the following tasks:

1. Create a table with two columns and four rows. In the first row, enter **Month** in the first cell and **Sales** in the second cell. Format these cells by using the **Heading 1** style.

2. In the second row, add the values **January** and **2,095**; in the third row, **February** and **3,478**; and in the fourth row, **March** and **2,561**.

3. Sort the table's rows in ascending order based on the values in the **Sales** column.

4. Add a table row with the values **April** and **1,702**.

5. Sort the bottom three rows in the table in descending order based on the values in the **Sales** column.

6. Change the background color of the **February** and **3,478** cells to yellow.

Attach files and printouts

Open the AttachFiles section in OneNote, and then perform the following tasks:

1. Attach the **LevelDescriptions** document to the active notebook page.

2. Edit the label of the attachment icon to read **Details on delivery service levels**.

3. Include the **LevelDescriptions** document as a printout on the same notebook page as the attachment.

4. Delete the attachment.

5. Save the printout file in the practice files folder with the new name **RevisedDescriptions**.

Add images and screen clippings

Open the AddImages section in OneNote, and then perform the following tasks:

1. Add the **WineryLandscape.jpg** image from the practice file folder to the active notebook page.

2. Move the image below the *Proposed Location* heading.

3. Resize the image so it is about half its original height and width.

4. Take a screen clipping of the structure in the middle of the photo and paste it just above the *Seating Capacity* text on the right side of the page.

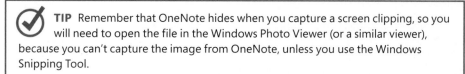

TIP Remember that OneNote hides when you capture a screen clipping, so you will need to open the file in the Windows Photo Viewer (or a similar viewer), because you can't capture the image from OneNote, unless you use the Windows Snipping Tool.

Create links to resources

Open the CreateLinks section in OneNote, and then perform the following tasks:

1. Select the *Official Microsoft OneNote site* text and use it as the base for a link to the web address **www.onenote.com**.

2. Click a blank spot on the page and create a link to the **LevelDescriptions** Word document in the practice file folder.

3. Click the link you just created to open the file.

4. Close the **LevelDescriptions** document, and then edit the text of the link to read **Service Level Details**.

Record audio and video notes

Open the RecordNotes section in OneNote, and then perform the following tasks:

1. Use the tools on the **Audio & Video** page of the **OneNote Options** dialog box to identify your audio and video inputs and the output formats you want to use.

2. Click below the *Audio Note* heading on the active notebook page.

3. Insert and record an audio note that is about 10 seconds in length, and then play it back.

4. Edit the audio note's label to reflect its contents.

5. Click below the *Video Note* heading.

6. Record a video note of about 10 seconds in length.

7. Play back the video note, pausing a few seconds into playback, and then restarting playback to let the note run to the end.

Insert time and date stamps

Open the InsertTimeStamps section in OneNote, and then perform the following tasks:

1. Next to the *Today's Date* text, insert a **Date** stamp.

2. Next to the *Current Time* text, insert a **Time** stamp.

3. Next to the *Document Review Completed* text, insert a **Date & Time** stamp.

Add symbols and equations

Open the AddSymbols section in OneNote, and then perform the following tasks:

1. From the gallery of common symbols, add a British pound currency symbol, £, to the left of the number **1450**.

2. Below the *Area of a Circle Formula* header, add the pre-built equation to calculate the area of a circle.

3. Below the *Additional Equation* header, create a custom equation that includes an exponent and an added constant value.

Add ink and shapes to a notebook

Typing notes into OneNote or a related app, such as Microsoft Word, is a terrific way to capture information. Even so, typing might not be your favorite way of taking down notes. If you want, you can enter content on a page by using touchscreen entry—often referred to as *ink entry mode*, or sometimes just *ink*—and then select, view, and erase the ink as needed. If your notes are text, you can convert your handwriting to text that can be copied and pasted among applications. You can also enter math equations by hand and have OneNote translate them into its internal language for representing math.

Finally, you can add shapes such as lines, polygons, and graph axes to your notebook by using a variety of built-in designs and styles. After you create these shapes, you can change their pen style to provide exactly the right appearance.

This chapter guides you through procedures related to adding notes by using ink; selecting, viewing, and erasing ink; converting ink to text and mathematical expressions; and creating and formatting shapes.

In this chapter

- Add notes by using ink
- Select, view, and erase ink
- Convert ink to text and mathematical expressions
- Create and format shapes

Practice files

For this chapter, use the practice files from the OneNoteSBS\Ch04 folder. For practice file download instructions, see the introduction.

Add notes by using ink

You can add text to a notebook page quickly when you use the keyboard, but it can be hard to switch from entering text to adding freehand diagrams and illustrations. If you are working on a touch-sensitive device, or you are comfortable drawing by using the mouse, a Surface Pen, or another input device, you can switch from keyboard input to ink.

When you switch over to ink entry mode, you select the pen color and line thickness you want to use. You can choose from a wide range of pen sizes and colors.

Add handwritten notes by using a variety of ink styles

> **TIP** If you use the mouse to draw or write, OneNote displays the pen point instead of the pointer. It can be hard to see the smaller pens, but you can quickly find the pen point by moving your mouse until the pen point leaves the surface of the page, when it turns back into the mouse pointer. The page navigation bar on the right side of the app window or the ribbon at the top are two convenient parts of the interface to use to locate the pen point.

The first six columns of the gallery contain pens that draw solid lines of varying color and thickness. Drawing a line by using any of those pens will write over any existing notebook contents. If you want to emphasize any of your notebook's contents, you can select one of the highlighter colors in the rightmost column of the gallery and draw on the page to highlight items on the page without obscuring the underlying contents.

When you want to change your pen, either to distinguish a new topic or just for a change of pace, you can select a new pen from the gallery or create a custom pen from the full range of colors and pen sizes, and you can specify whether you want to use a standard pen or a highlighter.

OneNote offers a number of modes for you to use when entering notes—which one you select depends on the type of notes you intend to create. OneNote distinguishes between handwriting and drawings—for example, when it offers to convert ink to text. The app interprets ink input as text or drawings, but you can specify whether OneNote should expect either type of input, only handwriting, or only drawings.

If you deliver a presentation based on a OneNote page, as you might in a study group, you can also use the pen as a pointer. You can indicate specific page content as if you were using a laser pointer, or draw temporary shapes or add text to help explain the page's contents. When you're done using any of the ink input or pointer modes, you can switch back to keyboard-based input.

To add an ink note by using a built-in pen style

1. On the **Draw** tab of the ribbon, in the **Tools** group, click a pen style in the **Pen Styles** gallery.

> **TIP** Click the More arrow in the lower-right corner of the Pen Styles gallery to display additional pens.

2. Use the mouse or, if you have a touch-sensitive device, a stylus, pen, or your finger to add ink to your page.

To emphasize page contents by using a highlighter

1. On the **Draw** tab, click one of the highlighter pen styles in the rightmost column of the **Pen Styles** gallery.

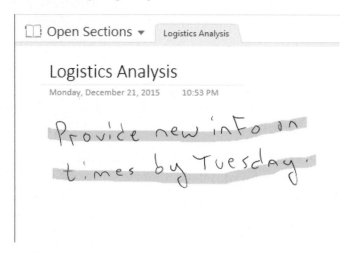

Emphasize page content by using a variety of highlighter colors

2. Use the mouse or, if you have a touch-sensitive device, a stylus, pen, or your finger to highlight items on your page.

> ⚠ **IMPORTANT** It can be tempting to use lots of highlighting, including multiple colors, to mark up your notes. Using too much color, or too many colors, can make your notebooks difficult to read. Apply highlighting wisely.

To change the active ink tool

1. Add ink to your page.

2. On the **Draw** tab, in the **Tools** group, click a different pen style in the **Pen Styles** gallery.

To create a custom ink tool

1. On the **Draw** tab, in the **Tools** group, click the **Color & Thickness** button.

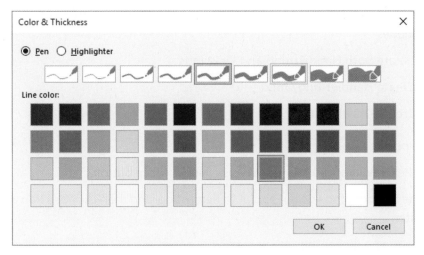

Apply detailed pen style settings by using the options in the Color & Thickness dialog box

2. In the **Color & Thickness** dialog box, do either of the following:

   - Select the **Pen** option to create a pen that draws with opaque color.

   - Select the **Highlighter** option to create a pen that draws with transparent color.

3. In the row of pen thicknesses, click the box representing the thickness of the line you want to apply.

4. In the **Line color** gallery, click the swatch representing the color you want to apply.

5. Click **OK**.

To select an ink input mode

1. On the **Draw** tab, click the **Pen Styles** gallery's **More** button.

2. At the bottom of the gallery, point to **Pen Mode**, and then click one of the following modes:

   - **Create Both Handwriting and Drawings**

   - **Create Handwriting Only**

   - **Create Drawings Only**

To use the pen as a pointer

1. On the **Draw** tab, click the **Pen Styles** gallery's **More** button.

2. At the bottom of the gallery, point to **Pen Mode**, and then click **Use Pen as Pointer**.

3. Move the pointer to indicate items on the page.

4. To mark a point on the screen, click the mouse button or, if you have a touchscreen, tap the screen with your finger or a stylus.

 TIP When you leave Ink mode, OneNote removes the ink you added while using the pen as a pointer.

To leave Ink mode and return to Type mode

1. On the **Draw** tab, in the **Tools** group, click the **Type** button.

   Or

   Press the **Esc** key.

Select, view, and erase ink

After you add ink content to a notebook by using the mouse, a stylus, or your finger, you can select the ink in preparation for editing. Due to the versatile nature of OneNote input, the standard rectangular selection area created by dragging the mouse pointer doesn't work well on most pages. To overcome that limitation, you can use the pointer to draw a border around the items you want to select by using the lasso tool.

Unlike physical pages, OneNote pages can be extended so that you can add notes below or to the right of the area displayed on screen when you first create the page. Moving within a page, or panning, lets you show page contents that are currently not displayed. If you pan away from the original page, or if you add items below or to the right of that original space, the horizontal and vertical scroll bars appear at the edges of the page display.

If you want to erase any of the ink items you've added to a page, you can select from several sizes of eraser to reflect the level of detail you want. You can also erase an entire stroke, which OneNote defines as a section of ink that was drawn without lifting your pen or finger, or releasing the mouse button.

4

 TIP If you activate the Stroke Eraser and click a line, such as an axis of a graph, that was created by the app, the Stroke Eraser acts like the Medium Eraser.

To select items by using lasso selection

1. On the **Draw** tab of the ribbon, in the **Tools** group, click **Lasso Select**.

2. On the active page, use the lasso to draw a border around the area of the page you want to select.

3. Cut or copy and move the selection as you would any other selected item in OneNote.

4. To return to Type mode, do either of the following:

   • On the **Draw** tab, click the **Type** button.

   • Press **Esc**.

To pan within a page

1. On the **Draw** tab, in the **Tools** group, click **Panning Hand**.

2. Drag the panning hand within the page to display parts of the page not currently shown within the app window.

3. To return to Type mode, do either of the following:

   • On the **Draw** tab, click the **Type** button.

   • Press **Esc**.

To erase ink

1. On the **Draw** tab, in the **Tools** group, click the **Eraser** button's arrow.

> **TIP** If you click the body of the Eraser button instead of the arrow, OneNote activates the last eraser you selected from the list.

2. In the list, click any of the following eraser types:

   - **Small Eraser**

   - **Medium Eraser**

   - **Large Eraser**

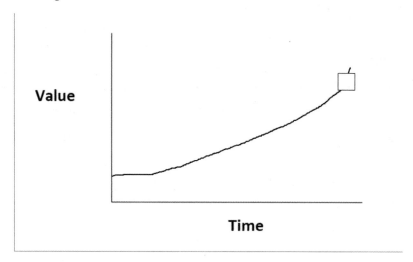

Erase ink by using a small, medium, or large eraser

3. To return to Type mode, do either of the following:

   - On the **Draw** tab, click the **Type** button.

   - Press **Esc**.

To erase entire strokes with one click

1. On the **Draw** tab, click the **Eraser** button's arrow, and then click **Stroke Eraser**.

2. Click anywhere on the stroke you want to erase, or click and drag the pointer over one or more strokes.

3. To return to Type mode, do either of the following:

   - On the **Draw** tab, click the **Type** button.

   - Press **Esc**.

Convert ink to text and mathematical expressions

4

Entering notes into a OneNote notebook by using ink combines the benefits of adding text in your own handwriting with the potential to convert your ink to text that is rendered by using a font such as Calibri or Times New Roman. After your text is represented by a font, you can check its spelling, translate words to other languages, and copy and paste the text within OneNote and to other applications.

 TIP You can copy and paste ink-based input to other programs, but those programs will treat the pasted item as an image.

If you use OneNote to take notes during classes, meetings, or project preparation and you need to record math equations, you can use ink to capture those equations in machine-readable form. Rather than write the formula on a page, you do so in a dialog box designed to facilitate math entry.

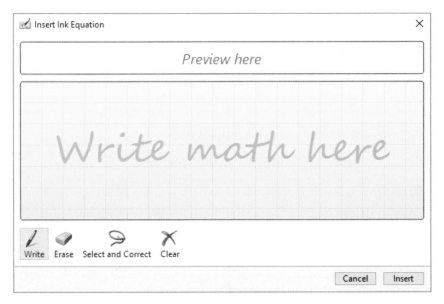

Add mathematical equations to your page by using ink

As you enter your equation, OneNote displays its current interpretation of your entry. The app's interpretation of your text might change as you write additional characters, so don't worry if one or two of the specific characters aren't exactly right at first. After you're done entering the equation, you can correct any remaining errors, delete and rewrite characters that OneNote can't figure out, or cancel the entry entirely.

 TIP You don't have to open the math entry dialog box to record an equation in OneNote. You can write the equation as regular ink, and then re-enter it when you have time after your class or meeting.

To convert ink to text

1. On a page, use ink to add handwriting to your notebook.

2. On the **Draw** tab of the ribbon, in the **Convert** group, click **Ink to Text**.

 TIP When you convert ink to text, OneNote styles the font with Calibri and the same color as the ink you used to write the note.

To convert ink to a mathematical expression

1. On the **Draw** tab, in the **Convert** group, click **Ink to Math**.

2. In the **Insert Ink Equation** dialog box, if necessary, click **Write**.

3. Use an ink input method to draw your mathematical expression in the **Write math here** box.

4. When you are done creating your equation, click **Insert**.

To erase part of an equation in the Insert Ink Equation dialog box

1. Start creating an equation in the **Insert Ink Equation** dialog box.

2. Click **Erase**.

3. Use the eraser to delete some of the writing from the **Write math here** area.

To correct how OneNote interprets your handwriting in the Insert Ink Equation dialog box

1. Start creating an equation in the **Insert Ink Equation** dialog box.

2. Click **Select and Correct**.

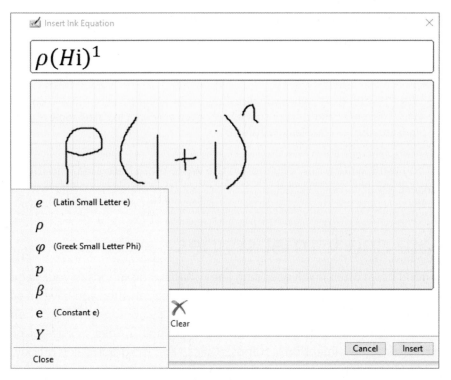

Correct how OneNote interprets your ink equations

3. Use the lasso selection tool to select the character or characters you want to correct.

4. Do either of the following:

   • From the list of suggestions that appears, click the correct character.

   • If none of the characters in the list are the one you want, click **Close**.

   > ⚠ **IMPORTANT** If OneNote doesn't suggest an appropriate replacement, try writing a few more characters to see if its interpretation improves. If it doesn't, erase the misinterpreted text and write the text you want to appear in a slightly different style to see if the change helps OneNote interpret your writing correctly.

5. If you have more to write, click **Write** and continue writing your equation.

6. Click **Insert**.

To clear the contents of the Insert Ink Equation dialog box

1. In the **Insert Ink Equation** dialog box in which an equation is already started in the **Write math here** area, click **Clear**.

> ⚠ **IMPORTANT** When you click Clear, your entire math equation will completely disappear, and you can't get it back. If you only want to delete some of your equation, use the Erase feature instead.

2. If you want, write a new equation in the **Write math here** area, and then click **Insert**.

Create and format shapes

Taking good notes often involves adding lines, shapes, and graphs to your page. For example, representing a timeline or process is much easier when you have an actual line to annotate. Basic shapes such as rectangles, ovals, rhombuses, triangles, and diamonds are available, and if you need to represent points, lines, or surfaces on two-dimensional or three-dimensional graphs, you can add the graph's axes quickly.

All of these items, collectively referred to as *shapes*, are available from within the OneNote app.

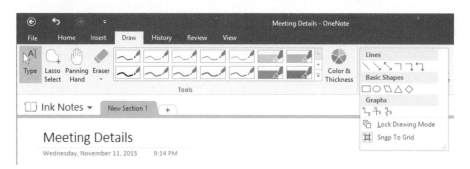

Select a line, polygon, or graph from the Shapes gallery

Initially the shape you add will take on the color and thickness of the currently selected pen. After you add a shape, you can change the color and thickness of the shape's lines, resize the shape, copy and paste it like any other item in OneNote, or move the shape to a new location on the current page. If you want to rotate or flip a shape, you can also do that. And, as with all OneNote items, you can delete any shapes you no longer need.

When you add shapes to a notebook page, OneNote puts each shape on its own layer. This means shapes are either in front of or behind other shapes on the page. For example, adding three shapes to a page would create three different layers.

4

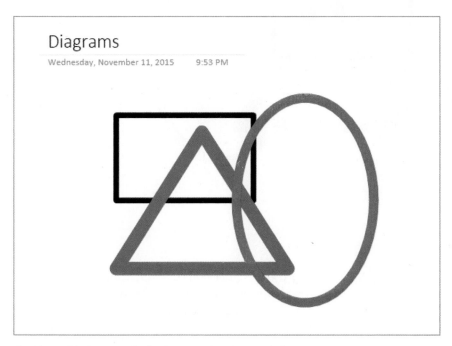

OneNote adds shapes and other items, such as images, in layers

You can change the order of shapes by moving individual shapes to different layers, such as by moving a shape to the front, up one level, down one level, or to the back.

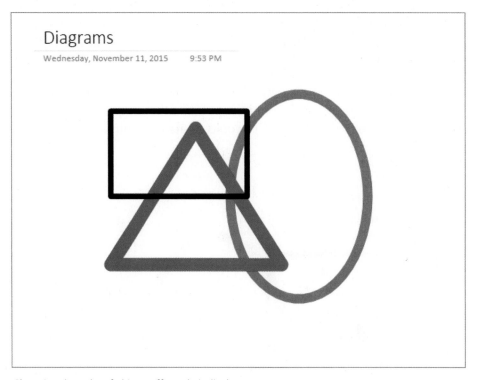

Changing the order of objects affects their display

When you add a shape, OneNote returns to the previous drawing mode after you release the mouse button. If you were panning around a page, for example, the panning tool would become active after you finish drawing the shape. You can lock drawing mode so that you can draw multiple shapes, and then you can unlock it again when you're done.

When you draw shapes on a page, it can be hard to get them to line up correctly. OneNote makes that task a bit easier by letting you align and draw objects by using a grid. The grid doesn't appear on the page, but you'll see lines and other shapes "snap" to the points on the grid. If you'd rather draw your shapes without the grid, you can turn it off.

Finally, OneNote offers an advantage that just isn't possible with paper: you can add more space to a page. For example, suppose you have two large groups of notes and you realize you left out some important information that really should go between the items. Rather than writing the new note elsewhere on the page and drawing an arrow to where it's supposed to go, you can add blank space to your page and separate the existing notes, so there's room to add new notes to complete your thought.

4

To add a line

1. On the **Draw** tab of the ribbon, in the **Shapes** gallery, click the line type you want to add.

2. On the page, click and drag in any direction to draw the line.

 TIP If the line has a bend in it, try dragging the line more vertically and horizontally to see the different ways in which you can extend the length of the two segments.

To add a polygon

1. On the **Draw** tab, in the **Shapes** gallery, click the polygon type you want to add.

2. On the page, click and drag in any direction to draw the polygon.

 TIP Try dragging your polygon in different directions. With some polygons, you can change their angles.

To add graph axes

1. On the **Draw** tab, in the **Shapes** gallery, click the graph axes type you want to add.

2. On the page, click and drag in any direction to draw the graph axes.

 TIP Try dragging the graph more vertically and horizontally to see the different ways in which you can extend the length of the axes.

To change the pen style of a shape

1. With the **Type** button on the **Draw** tab selected, click the shape to select it.

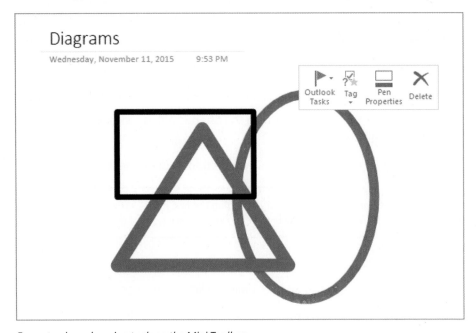

Format a shape by using tools on the Mini Toolbar

2. On the Mini Toolbar that appears, click **Pen Properties**.

3. Select **Pen** to create a pen that draws with an opaque color.

   Or

   Select **Highlighter** to create a pen that draws with a transparent color.

4. In the row of pen thicknesses, click the box representing the thickness of the line you want to apply.

5. In the **Line color** gallery, click the square representing the color you want to apply.

6. Click **OK**.

To resize a shape

1. With the **Type** button on the **Draw** tab selected, click the shape to select it.

2. Point to one of the handles on the shape's sides or corners, and drag the handle to resize the shape.

To move a shape

1. With the **Type** button on the **Draw** tab selected, click the shape to select it.

2. Point to the body of the shape. When the pointer changes to a four-headed arrow, drag the shape to its new location.

To rotate a shape

1. Select the shape you want to rotate.

2. On the **Draw** tab, in the **Edit** group, click the **Rotate** button, and then click the command that represents how you want to rotate the shape.

To delete a shape

1. Select the shape.

2. Do either of the following:

   • On the **Draw** tab, in the **Edit** group, click **Delete**.

   • On the Mini Toolbar that appears, click **Delete**.

   • Press **Delete**.

To arrange shapes

1. Select the shapes you want to arrange.

2. On the **Draw** tab, in the **Edit** group, click the **Arrange** button, and then click the command (**Bring Forward**, **Bring to Front**, **Send Backward**, or **Send to Back**) that reflects how you want to move the shape.

To lock or unlock drawing mode

1. On the **Draw** tab, click the **Shapes** gallery's **More** button, and then click **Lock Drawing Mode**.

>   **TIP** As its name implies, after you Lock Drawing Mode, you can freely move around to use the different pens and shapes without worrying about OneNote snapping back to Type mode. Just click the Type button on the Draw tab when you're done.

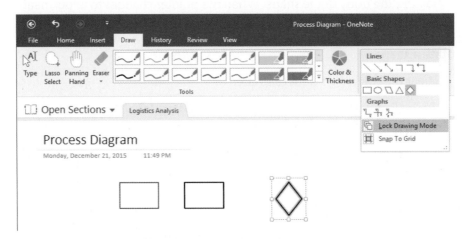

Create multiple shapes by clicking Lock Drawing Mode

To turn Snap To Grid on or off

1. On the **Draw** tab, click the **Shapes** gallery's **More** button, and then click **Snap To Grid**.

> **TIP** Turning Snap To Grid off will give you more control over your shape, but it could be much faster to snap your shape to a grid when you move or resize it.

To insert space on a page

1. On the **Draw** tab, in the **Edit** group, click **Insert Space**.

2. Point to the area of the page where you want to add space. A large arrow appears. Move the pointer until the arrow points in the direction (up, down, left, or right) that you want to drag to insert space into the page.

3. Drag the pointer to add space to the page.

Skills review

In this chapter, you learned how to:

- Add notes by using ink
- Select, view, and erase ink
- Convert ink to text and mathematical expressions
- Create and format shapes

4

Practice tasks

The practice files for these tasks are located in the OneNoteSBS\Ch04 folder. The results of the tasks will be automatically saved into the same file in the same folder.

Add notes by using ink

Open the AddInkNotes section in OneNote, and then perform the following tasks:

1. On the active notebook page, use the tools on the **Draw** tab of the ribbon to click a pen style in the gallery and, below the *Verify Project Due Date* header, write a note indicating that the project is due two weeks from the current day.

2. Change the pen to a yellow highlighter and highlight the text *Send to manager for review two days prior to final submission*.

3. Create a custom pen style and add a note to remind yourself to ask whether or not the project deadline will be extended.

Select, view, and erase ink

Open the SelectInk section in OneNote, and then perform the following tasks:

1. Use the **Panning Hand** to pan to the right and display the handwritten table of transit times.

2. Using **Lasso Select**, select the handwritten table and drag it to the left to position it underneath the text that reads *Average transit time for last two months has fallen to 24 days. Revise our model?*

3. Using the **Large Eraser**, erase the handwritten text that says *Bring over new transit data*.

Convert ink to text and mathematical expressions

Open the ConvertInk section in OneNote, and then perform the following tasks:

1. On the page, use ink to write **This equation calculates the value of an invest-ment subject to compound interest** and convert the ink to text.

2. Use the **Insert Ink Equation** dialog box to enter the formula displayed on the page as an ink equation.

Create and format shapes

Open the FormatShapes section in OneNote, and then perform the following tasks:

1. Using the tools on the **Draw** tab of the ribbon, draw an arrow from the text that reads *Is there a due date for this project?* to the text that reads *Due date con-firmed: April 14.*

2. Add a square or rectangle around the *Due date confirmed: April 14* text.

3. Change the pen color and thickness of the box you drew around the text.

4. Move the box behind the arrowed line you drew in step 1.

Review and password-protect notebook text

5

Taking notes is a surprisingly involved task. Not only do you have to listen to or watch the content you're taking notes on, you have to record a summary of what is being said or done. When you write or type that quickly, it's likely you will make spelling mistakes. If you want to improve your notebook's text, you can do so by checking its spelling. The spelling checker comes with a good general dictionary, but you can add any words it doesn't know so it recognizes them, rather than asking you if you want to change them.

Related tools include AutoCorrect options, which make automatic changes based on rules you can control, and tools that translate text between languages, research words or phrases you might not be familiar with, and look up word alternatives in a thesaurus. Finally, if your notebook contains data you don't want other people to be able to read, you can add password protection to notebook sections.

This chapter guides you through procedures related to checking spelling, setting AutoCorrect options, translating and researching text, and password-protecting sections.

In this chapter

- Check spelling
- Set AutoCorrect options
- Translate and research text
- Password-protect sections

Practice files

For this chapter, use the practice files from the OneNoteSBS\Ch05 folder. For practice file download instructions, see the introduction.

Check spelling

When you take notes during a meeting or class, you probably write or type quickly to ensure that you capture all of the information you can. Those notes might contain misspelled words, which isn't a big problem if you work through your own notes but can make it harder for your colleagues to understand exactly what you mean.

You can check the spelling of the words in your notebook to improve the notes you take. When the OneNote spelling checker encounters a word that isn't in the dictionary, it presents a series of choices you can select from.

OneNote suggests replacement words for misspellings

The built-in dictionaries are meant for general writers, so it's likely you will use some words that don't appear in the OneNote dictionaries. If that's the case, you can have OneNote ignore that word for the rest of the current spelling check operation or, if you think you will use the word in other documents, you can add it to the dictionary. When OneNote flags a misspelled word in your notebook and you're unsure how to pronounce it, you can play an audio clip of the word's standard pronunciation.

There are a number of ways you can control how OneNote checks spelling in your notebooks. One way is to change the language used in the spelling check operation. If you find that you use a lot of words in a language other than the language specified in your Windows regional settings (such as English or Spanish), you can change to the language you need to check individual words or the entire text of the section.

You can also use custom dictionaries to check the spelling of your document. Custom dictionaries contain words that might not appear in a standard language dictionary. You can edit the word list of a custom dictionary to add words that might appear in your specific context, such as an engineering notebook, but not in all situations.

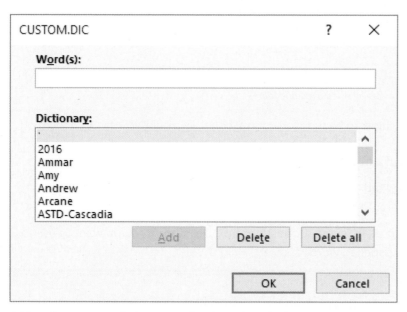

Add words to a custom dictionary to refine the spelling checker

Because OneNote is part of the Microsoft Office family of apps, you can change the spelling check options for every Office app from within OneNote. Those options include ignoring words that appear in all uppercase, ignoring words that contain numbers, and ignoring repeated words. Depending on the work you do, all of those options could improve your experience.

Finally, OneNote and other Office applications, such as Microsoft Word, indicate words that might be spelled incorrectly or that might represent improper grammar. Suspected misspelled words are underlined in red, and suspected grammar errors are underlined in blue.

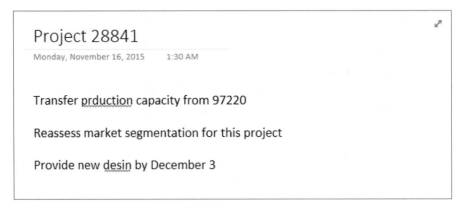

OneNote marks spelling errors by using a red underline

If you find those indicators to be more of a distraction than a help, you can turn them off.

To check spelling on a notebook page

1. On the **Review** tab of the ribbon, in the **Spelling** group, click the **Spelling** button to open the Spelling pane.

2. In the **Spelling** pane, in the suggestions box, click the word you want to use to replace the misspelled word.

3. Click **Change**.

4. Repeat steps 1–3 until you have checked the entire page.

5. In the dialog box that opens, click **OK**.

To ignore a flagged word without adding it to a dictionary

1. With the flagged word displayed in the **Spelling** pane, click the **Ignore** button.

To add a flagged word to the custom dictionary

1. Do either of the following:

   • With the flagged word displayed in the **Spelling** pane, click the **Add** button.

   • Right-click a misspelled word that has a red underline, and then click **Add to Dictionary**.

To play an audio file demonstrating the pronunciation of a flagged word

1. With the flagged word displayed in the **Spelling** pane, click the sound icon next to the word below the suggestions box.

2. If you want, click any of the words in the suggestions box to display it instead of the flagged word below the box, and then click the sound icon next to the new word to play an audio file of its pronunciation.

To change the language used in the spelling check operation

1. Start the spelling checker.

2. In the **Spelling** pane, click the language list arrow, and then click the language you want to use for the spelling check.

> ⚠ **IMPORTANT** This change persists beyond the current spelling check. For example, if you normally use the English (United States) dictionary but switch to the English (United Kingdom) dictionary to check the spelling of a notebook, that dictionary remains as the dictionary setting for all of your notebooks until you change back to English (United States).

To use custom dictionaries when checking spelling

1. Click the **File** tab of the ribbon to display the Backstage view.

2. In the Backstage view, click **Options** at the bottom of the left pane.

3. In the **OneNote Options** dialog box, click **Proofing** in the left pane.

4. On the **Proofing** page of the dialog box, in the **When correcting spelling in Microsoft Office programs** section, click **Custom Dictionaries**.

5. In the **Custom Dictionaries** dialog box, select the check box next to any dictionary you want to use.

> **TIP** When it checks your spelling, the spelling checker uses all the dictionaries that have their check boxes selected. Browse through the different dictionaries to see what the spelling checker is checking.

6. Click **OK**.

To edit the word list of a custom dictionary

1. On the **Proofing** page of the **OneNote Options** dialog box, in the **When correcting spelling in Microsoft Office programs** section, click **Custom Dictionaries**.

2. In the **Custom Dictionaries** dialog box, click the custom dictionary you want to edit.

3. Click **Edit Word List**.

4. In the custom dictionary dialog box, perform any of the following tasks:

    -   In the **Word(s)** box, enter a new word and then click **Add**.

    -   In the **Dictionary** box, click a term and then click **Delete**.

    -   Click **Delete all** to delete all of the words in the custom dictionary.

5. Click **OK** to close the editing dialog box.

6. Click **OK** to close the Custom Dictionaries dialog box.

7. Click **OK** to close the OneNote Options dialog box.

To set spelling options for all Office apps

1. In the **OneNote Options** dialog box, click **Proofing**.

2. On the **Proofing** page of the dialog box, in the **When correcting spelling in Microsoft Office programs** section, select or clear the check boxes for any of the following rules:

    -   **Ignore words in UPPERCASE**

    -   **Ignore words that contain numbers**

- **Ignore Internet and file addresses**

- **Flag repeated words**

- **Enforce accented uppercase in French**

- **Suggest from main dictionary only**

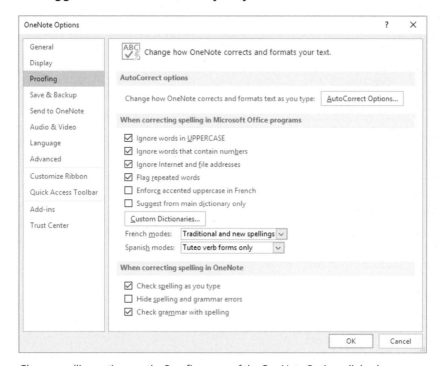

Change spelling options on the Proofing page of the OneNote Options dialog box

3. Click **OK** to close the OneNote Options dialog box.

To turn off checking spelling as you type

1. On the **Proofing** page of the **OneNote Options** dialog box, in the **When correcting spelling in OneNote** section, clear the **Check spelling as you type** check box.

2. Click **OK**.

Set AutoCorrect options

Humans are creatures of habit. We often misspell words in the same way, such as substituting *teh* for *the*. OneNote has a built-in set of rules, called AutoCorrect rules, that it uses to correct what it believes are misspelled words. If you want to review the AutoCorrect rules OneNote applies, you can take a look at the list.

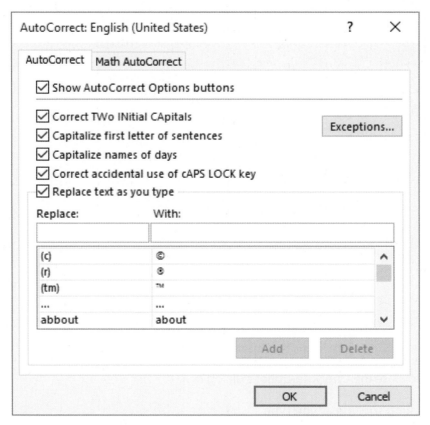

Change common typing errors by using AutoCorrect

If you find that you misspell words in ways that aren't on the list, you can create your own AutoCorrect rule. AutoCorrect might also change some words or acronyms that you are using correctly. In that case, you can delete the rule so it doesn't affect your work.

> **TIP** If you often enter a particular block of text, such as a street address, you can create a nonsense word that serves as a code for the standard block of text you want to enter, and you can create an AutoCorrect rule that causes OneNote to automatically replace that word with the text block.

In addition to correcting misspelled words or phrases, AutoCorrect also corrects common typing errors such as not capitalizing the first letter of a sentence and starting words with two initial capital letters. You can also decide whether to have AutoCorrect correct your text as you type. If you turn off AutoCorrect, OneNote doesn't apply any of the rules to your notes' text.

For users who add mathematical expressions to their notebooks, OneNote also offers AutoCorrect replacements for math expressions.

5

Add math expressions by taking advantage of Math AutoCorrect

If you plan to use Math AutoCorrect, you should look through the list of text and replacement value pairs to determine the values you might use as part of your projects at school or work.

To add an AutoCorrect rule

1. Click the **File** tab of the ribbon to display the Backstage view, and then click **Options**.

2. In the **OneNote Options** dialog box, click **Proofing**.

3. On the **Proofing** page of the **OneNote Options** dialog box, in the **AutoCorrect options** section, click the **AutoCorrect Options** button.

4. In the **AutoCorrect** dialog box, in the **Replace** box, enter the value for which you want to define an AutoCorrect replacement (for example, you can enter *e-mail*).

5. In the **With** box, enter the value you want to use to replace the text in the **Replace** box (for example, you can enter *email*).

6. Click **Add** to add the AutoCorrect replacement rule.

7. Click **OK** to close the AutoCorrect dialog box.

8. Click **OK** to close the OneNote Options dialog box.

To delete an AutoCorrect rule

1. On the **Proofing** page of the **OneNote Options** dialog box, in the **AutoCorrect options** section, click the **AutoCorrect Options** button.

2. In the **AutoCorrect** dialog box, in the list of **Replace** and **With** pairs, click the entry you want to delete.

> **TIP** You can start typing in the Replace box to make the scrollable window jump down to the word that is to be replaced.

3. Click the **Delete** button.

4. Click **OK** to close the AutoCorrect dialog box.

5. Click **OK** to close the OneNote Options dialog box.

To undo an AutoCorrect action

1. After OneNote makes an AutoCorrect change to your text, point to the small rectangular indicator that appears below the corrected text to display the AutoCorrect Options action button.

> Will be able to use knowledge of data structures in other work, so overall a very good win.
>
> Try to accommodate

An AutoCorrect indicator appears below a change (in this case, below the word accommodate)

2. In the list, click any of these options:

   - **Change back to text**, which restores the original text

   - **Stop automatically correcting text**, which deletes the rule

   - **Control AutoCorrect Options**, which opens the AutoCorrect dialog box

To control AutoCorrect actions

1. On the **Proofing** page of the **OneNote Options** dialog box, in the **AutoCorrect options** section, click the **AutoCorrect Options** button.

2. In the **AutoCorrect** dialog box, select or clear any of these check boxes:

   - **Correct TWo INitial CApitals**

   - **Capitalize first letter of sentences**

   - **Capitalize names of days**

   - **Correct accidental use of cAPS LOCK key**

   - **Replace text as you type**

3. Click **OK** to close the AutoCorrect dialog box.

4. Click **OK** to close the OneNote Options dialog box.

To define exceptions to AutoCorrect rules

1. On the **Proofing** page of the **OneNote Options** dialog box, in the **AutoCorrect options** section, click the **AutoCorrect Options** button.

2. In the **AutoCorrect** dialog box, click the **Exceptions** button to open the AutoCorrect Exceptions dialog box.

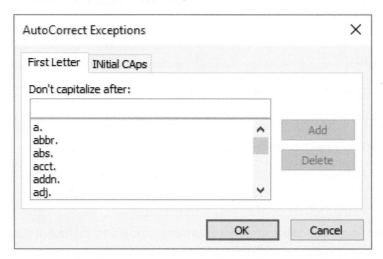

Create exceptions for AutoCorrect's automatic capitalization at the start of a sentence

3. Do either of the following:

   - On the **First Letter** tab, enter your text in the **Don't capitalize after** box, click the **Add** button, and then click **OK**.

   - On the **INitial CAps** tab, enter your text in the **Don't correct** box, click the **Add** button, and then click **OK**.

4. Click **OK** to close the **AutoCorrect** dialog box.

5. Click **OK** to close the **OneNote Options** dialog box.

> **TIP** To delete an exception, display it in the box near the top of the AutoCorrect Exceptions dialog box, click Delete, and then click OK to close the dialog box.

To define math-related AutoCorrect rules

1. On the **Proofing** page of the **OneNote Options** dialog box, in the **AutoCorrect options** section, click the **AutoCorrect Options** button.

2. In the **AutoCorrect** dialog box, click the **Math AutoCorrect** tab.

3. On the **Math AutoCorrect** tab, in the **Replace** box, enter the text you want to replace with a mathematical entry.

4. In the **With** box, enter the math symbol or symbols you want to use to replace the text in the Replace box.

5. Click the **Add** button.

6. Click **OK** to close the AutoCorrect dialog box.

7. Click **OK** to close the OneNote Options dialog box.

Translate and research text

As communication at work and school becomes more international, the need to translate text from your primary language to other languages takes on more importance. In OneNote, you can translate words or phrases to other languages. When the cursor is positioned within a word, you can use the shortcut menu to have OneNote translate it. If you turn on the Mini Translator, pointing to a word displays its translation.

> **TIP** OneNote provides a list of possible translations for the word or phrase you ask it to translate. For example, the English word *bell* can be translated several different ways into French, depending on whether the bell is a bicycle bell, a church bell, or something else. Look through the options presented to determine the best fit for your context.

If you want to work regularly in a language other than the one specified in your Windows regional settings, you can change the language OneNote uses for handwriting recognition and for proofing tools such as those that check spelling and grammar.

You can also look up words by using the Encarta dictionary and an online thesaurus. These research tools can be especially helpful for text you have copied into your notebook from an external source for later review, or to remind yourself of the meaning of a term you might not have worked with for a while.

 TIP Both the dictionary and thesaurus are available in multiple languages.

OneNote has access to a wide range of research services, including online sources of information, that you can make available by setting the app's research options to allow their use.

To translate selected text to another language

1. Select the text you want to translate.

2. Do either of the following:

   - On the **Review** tab of the ribbon, in the **Language** group, click **Translate**, and then click **Translate Selected Text**.

   - Right-click the selected text, and click **Translate**.

3. The Translate Selected Text dialog box opens, indicating that your search terms will be sent in secure form to an external server. Click **Yes**. The Research pane opens.

 TIP To avoid having to perform this step in the Translate Selected Text dialog box in the future, click Don't Show Again before you click Yes.

If the word you want to look up doesn't appear in your notebook, you can enter it in the Search For box at the top of the Research pane

4. In the **Research** pane, if necessary, click the **From** list arrow, and then click the language of the word or phrase.

5. If necessary, click the **To** list arrow, and then click the language to which you want to translate the word or phrase. The translation is displayed in the Research pane's content area.

6. If you want to translate a different word, change the text in the **Search for** box, and click the **Start searching** button (which looks like a right-pointing white arrow in a green square next to the **Search for** box at the top of the pane).

> ✓ **TIP** You don't need to click the Start Searching button when the Research pane opens or when you switch the translation languages. The translation results are displayed automatically. However, if you change the text in the Search For box, you'll need to click the Start Searching button to display the translation results.

To use the Mini Translator

1. On the **Review** tab, in the **Language** group, click **Translate**, and then click **Mini Translator**.

2. If this is your first use of the Mini Translator, the Translation Language Options dialog box opens. Select the language you want to translate to, and then click **OK**.

3. The Mini Translator dialog box opens, indicating that your search terms will be sent in secure form to an external server. (If you want to avoid this dialog box in the future, select the **Don't show again** check box.) Click **Yes** to close the dialog box. The Mini Translator is turned on.

To read and review a translation by using the Mini Translator

1. With the Mini Translator turned on, point to the word that you want to translate.

2. Point to the semi-transparent **Bilingual Dictionary** dialog box to review the translation.

3. Click the **Expand** button (a magnifying glass in front of two books) to open the Research pane with the word and its translation displayed.

To change the translation language used by the translator tools

1. On the **Review** tab, in the **Language** group, click **Translate**, and then click **Choose Translation Language**.

2. In the **Translation Language Options** dialog box, select the new language, and then click **OK**.

To change the language used by handwriting recognition and the proofing tools

1. On the **Review** tab, in the **Language** group, click the **Language** button, and then click **Set Proofing Language**.

2. In the **Proofing Language** pane, in the **Pick language** list, click the language to use for handwriting recognition and proofing tools.

3. At the right edge of the **Proofing Language** pane's title bar, click the **Close** button.

To look up a word in the Encarta dictionary

1. Select the word you want to look up.

2. On the **Review** tab, in the **Spelling** group, click **Research**.

3. In the **Research** pane, click the resource list arrow, and then click **Encarta Dictionary**.

To replace a word with a word from a thesaurus

1. Select the word you want to look up.

2. On the **Review** tab, in the **Spelling** group, click **Thesaurus**.

3. To replace the word with a synonym, point to the synonym, click the arrow that appears next to the synonym, and then click **Insert**.

To paste in a synonym in a different place on the page

1. Select the word you want to look up.

2. On the **Review** tab, in the **Spelling** group, click **Thesaurus**.

3. Point to the synonym, click the arrow that appears next to the synonym, and then click **Copy**.

4. Paste the word where you want it on your OneNote page.

 TIP To look up another word, enter it in the Thesaurus box and click the search button or press Enter.

5. Click the **Close** button to close the Thesaurus pane.

To set research options

1. On the **Review** tab, in the **Spelling** group, click **Research**.

2. At the bottom of the **Research** pane, click **Research options**.

3. In the **Research Options** dialog box, do any of the following:

    - In the **Services** pane, select or clear check boxes to enable the services you want to be available within OneNote.

    - Below the **Services** pane, click the **Add Services** button to add the URL of a provider as a research option. In the **Add Services** dialog box, in the **Address** box, enter the provider's URL. Click **Add**, and then click **Close** to return to the Research Options dialog box.

    - Below the **Services** pane, click the **Update/Remove** button to update or remove any of the currently installed services. In the **Update or Remove Services** dialog box, in the list (grouped by provider), select the service you want to update or remove, such as Microsoft Translator and Bing. Click **Update** or **Remove**, and then click **Close** to return to the Research Options dialog box.

    - Below the **Services** pane, click the **Parental Control** button to set parental controls for use of these services.

     TIP To access the parental control settings, you must be logged on as an administrator or as another account that's allowed to modify the settings.

4. Click **OK** to change the settings and close the Research Options dialog box.

Password-protect sections

OneNote is a terrific app for sharing ideas with your classmates and colleagues, but not every piece of information you record in a notebook should be available for everyone to read. Some data might provide insights into your company's plans and costs, and other bits of information could include names and addresses of friends or colleagues you don't care to share with other individuals who could have access to other pages in your notebook.

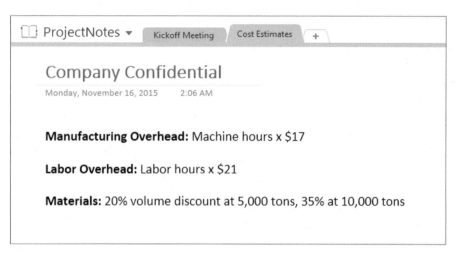

Confidential information isn't always marked confidential...be careful!

Setting a password for a section requires users to enter the password any time the section is locked, which can occur after a period of inactivity, if the user closes and then reopens the notebook, or if you manually lock all password-protected sections in the notebook.

> **TIP** The best passwords are long passwords with a mix of uppercase letters, lowercase letters, numbers, and symbols. If you have a hard time remembering a password with mixes of the four character types, consider using a password management program, or use a series of four or five medium-length words. In general, though, the longer your password, the better.

After you set a password for a section, you can enter the password to display the section, change the password, remove the password, and set password options. One option you might set is to have OneNote lock a password-protected section when you navigate away from it (that is, when you display another section). Turning on this option requires you to enter a section's password every time you display it, which is a bit of work, but it might be worth it if the section contains sensitive information.

To assign a password to a section

1. Display the section you want to protect by clicking its tab.

2. On the **Review** tab of the ribbon, in the **Section** group, click the **Password** button to open the Password Protection pane.

3. In the **Password Protection** pane, click the **Set Password** button.

Add a password to protect a section's contents

4. In the **Enter Password** box, enter the password you want to apply to the section.

5. In the **Confirm Password** box, re-enter the password.

> **TIP** OneNote passwords help protect your notebook's sections, but they are difficult if not impossible to recover if you forget them. To avoid losing access to your data, make sure you can remember your password or write it down.

6. Click **OK**.

> **IMPORTANT** If OneNote has created backup copies of the protected section, the Existing Section Backups dialog box appears. Click Delete Existing Backups to erase these backup copies, which are not password protected, or click Keep Existing Backups to retain the unprotected sections.

To display a password-protected section

1. Click the tab of the protected section.

2. Click the body of the section.

   Or

   Press **Enter**.

Enter a section's password to display its contents

3. In the **Protected Section** dialog box, in the **Enter Password** box, enter the section's password.

4. Click **OK**.

To lock all sections that have had passwords assigned

1. Do either of the following:

   • In the **Password Protection** pane, click **Lock All**.

   • Press **Ctrl+Alt+L**.

To change a section password

1. Click the tab of the protected section.

2. If necessary, on the **Review** tab, in the **Section** group, click **Password** to open the Password Protection pane.

3. In the **Password Protection** pane, click **Change Password**.

4. In the **Old Password** box, enter the existing password for the section.

5. In the **Enter New Password** box, enter the new password you want to apply to the section.

6. In the **Confirm Password** box, re-enter the new password.

7. Click **OK**.

To set password options

1. At the bottom of the **Password Protection** pane, click **Password Options** to open the OneNote Options dialog box with the Advanced page displayed.

2. On the **Advanced** page of the **OneNote Options** dialog box, scroll down to the **Passwords** section.

3. Perform any of the following actions to change password options:

   - Select or clear the **Lock password protected sections after I have not worked in them for the following amount of time** check box, and then click the **Interval** list arrow and select the amount of time.

   - Select or clear the **Lock password protected sections as soon as I navigate away from them** check box to control whether OneNote locks a protected section as soon as you move to another section.

   - Select or clear the **Enable add-in programs to access password protected sections when they are unlocked** check box to control these programs' access to password-protected sections.

4. Click **OK**.

To remove a password from a section

1. Display the section and, if necessary, enter the password needed to display its contents.

2. If necessary, on the **Review** tab, in the **Section** group, click **Password** to open the Password Protection pane.

3. In the **Password Protection** pane, click **Remove Password**.

4. In the **Remove Password** dialog box, enter the current password.

5. Click **OK**.

5

Skills review

In this chapter, you learned how to:

- Check spelling

- Set AutoCorrect options

- Translate and research text

- Password-protect sections

Practice tasks

The practice files for these tasks are located in the OneNoteSBS\Ch05 folder. The results of the tasks will be automatically saved into the same file in the same folder.

Check spelling

Open the CheckSpelling section in OneNote, and then perform the following tasks:

1. Start the spelling checker, and replace the first misspelled word with the word *production*.

2. Add the second highlighted word, *resegmentation*, to the custom dictionary.

3. Replace the last misspelled word with the correct word, *Provide*.

4. Right-click the section tab, and then click **Close**.

Set AutoCorrect options

Open the SetAutoCorrectOptions section in OneNote, and then perform the following tasks:

1. Under the **Customer Status** label, enter **nwe**, which OneNote will change to *New*.

2. Add a new AutoCorrect entry that replaces the text **tbh** with the text **Order to be held in the warehouse until final credit approval comes through**.

3. In the body of the OneNote page, enter **tbh** followed by a space.

Translate and research text

Open the TranslateText section in OneNote, and then perform the following tasks:

1. On the page, turn on the Mini Translator, click within the word *volume*, and translate the word from English to German.

2. Look up the word *volume* in the Encarta dictionary, and then look for alternative words and phrases in the thesaurus.

Password-protect sections

Open the ProtectSections section in OneNote, and then perform the following tasks:

1. Set a password for the **ProtectSections** section in the file. For the purposes of this test, make it a short word or number string such as **123**.

2. Lock the section manually.

3. Unlock the **ProtectSections** section.

4. Remove the password from the protected section.

Manage views, windows, and page versions

6

As you work with OneNote, you will probably create notebook pages with a lot of content. Whatever those notes are related to—business, school, community, or other organizational projects—there will be times when you will want to show as much of the page as possible. You can change the page's view to hide the ribbon, or you can dock a page to the side of your screen so it's always available. You can also zoom in or out on the page to show more or less of its contents, or change your page's size, background color, and lines.

When you collaborate with your colleagues on a notebook, you will probably be interested in reviewing notes by author, and you can have OneNote indicate the notes that are unread. You can perform both of those tasks, in addition to keeping a record of different versions of your pages over time. Maintaining a history of a notebook section lets you look back for items that might have been deleted. You can also delete individual page versions or stop maintaining notebook history altogether if you want to.

This chapter guides you through procedures related to managing notebook views and links, extending your view by zooming and adding windows, controlling page setup, reviewing notes by author and read status, and managing page versions and history.

In this chapter

- Manage notebook views and links

- Extend your view by zooming and adding windows

- Control page setup

- Review notes by author and read status

- Manage page versions and history

Practice files

For this chapter, use the practice files from the OneNoteSBS\Ch06 folder. For practice file download instructions, see the introduction.

Manage notebook views and links

When you take notes in OneNote, the app runs as a standard app on your computer or other device. If you don't change anything, your notebook appears in Normal view, which includes the ribbon, app window, and window controls. If you need more room to work, you can display your notebook in Full Page view, which hides the ribbon and navigation tools.

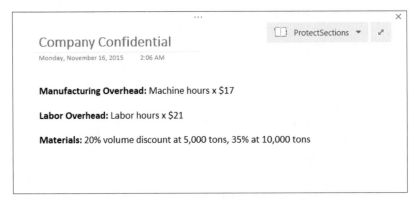

Maximize available space by using Full Page view

Another way to work with a OneNote window is to dock it to the desktop. Docking a OneNote window creates a space that stays active and visible regardless of the other apps you open.

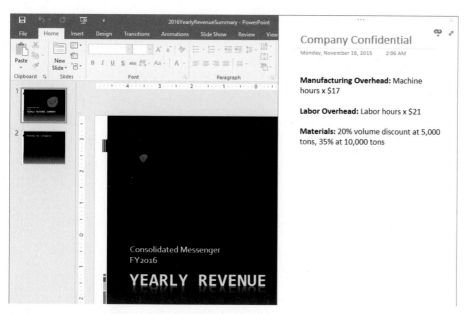

Dock a OneNote window to keep it visible at all times

While you have a docked window open, you can create linked notes. A linked note refers to files other than the current OneNote notebook. If your page contains linked notes, you can view the files to which you have created links, delete individual links, delete all links, or stop creating linked notes entirely. You can also set your linked note options to control how OneNote handles linked notes going forward.

 SEE ALSO For more information about links, which can include hyperlinks to web resources, see "Create links to resources" in Chapter 3, "Work with your notes."

To display a page in Normal view

1. Do either of the following:

   - If the ribbon is available, on the **View** tab of the ribbon, in the **Views** group, click the **Normal View** button.

   - In any view that does not display the ribbon, click the **Normal View** button in the upper-right corner.

To display a page in Full Page view

1. Do either of the following:

   - On the **View** tab, in the **Views** group, click the **Full Page View** button.

   - In Normal view, click the **Full Page View** button (the diagonal double-headed arrow) in the upper-right corner of the page.

To display the ribbon in Full Page view

1. Click the ellipse at the top of the app window.

 TIP When you are done using the ribbon, click any spot on the page to hide it.

To dock the OneNote window to the desktop

1. On the **View** tab, in the **Views** group, click the **Dock to Desktop** button.

To display the ribbon in a docked window

1. Click the ellipse at the top of the docked window.

To create a linked note

1. With a OneNote window docked to the desktop, open the file you want to link to (for example, a webpage in Microsoft Edge or Internet Explorer, a Word document, a PowerPoint presentation, or another OneNote notebook).

2. Create a note in the docked window.

 TIP When you create a linked note, a link to the corresponding app and an icon representing the app appear next to the note when you point to it.

To identify files linked to linked notes

1. In a docked OneNote window, click the **Linked Note Taking** button near the upper-right corner of the window.

2. In the list, point to **Linked File(s)**, and then click the file you want to display.

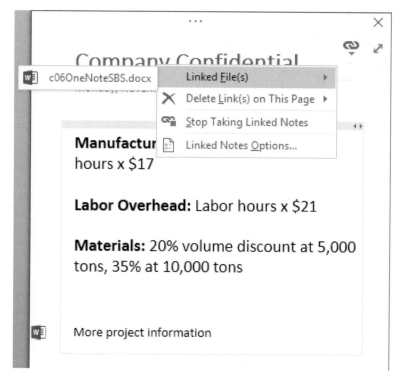

Display a list of linked files in a docked window

3. Do the following:

   - For links to Word and PowerPoint files, read the text in the warning dialog box that appears. If you trust the file to which OneNote is linked, click **OK**.

   - For links to OneNote pages, read the text in the security notice dialog box that appears. If you trust the OneNote file, click **Yes**.

 TIP Links to webpages that open in Internet Explorer or Microsoft Edge don't require you to confirm access.

To delete links in a docked OneNote window

1. In the docked window, click the **Linked Note Taking** button near the upper-right corner of the window, and point to **Delete Link(s) on This Page**.

2. Do either of the following:

   - Click the file whose link you want to delete.

   - Click **Delete All Links on This Page**.

To stop taking linked notes

1. In a docked OneNote window, click the **Linked Note Taking** button near the upper-right corner of the window.

2. In the list, click **Stop Taking Linked Notes**.

> ✓ **TIP** When you click Stop Taking Linked Notes, the notes you add in the docked window will no longer create links. The Linked Note Taking button changes to show you that it is turned off.

To set linked note options

1. In a docked OneNote window, click the **Linked Note Taking** button near the upper-right corner of the window, and then click **Linked Notes Options** to display the Linked Notes section of the Advanced page of the OneNote Options dialog box.

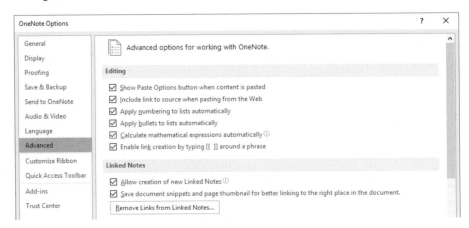

Manage linked note options in the OneNote Options dialog box

2. In the **OneNote Options** dialog box, do any of the following:

   - Select or clear the **Allow creation of new Linked Notes** check box.

   - Select or clear the **Save document snippets and page thumbnail for better linking to the right place in the document** check box.

   - Click **Remove Links from Linked Notes**, and then, in the confirmation dialog box, click **Remove**.

3. Click **OK**.

Extend your view by zooming and adding windows

Every page in a OneNote notebook contains information related to a specific subject. If one of your pages is so large that it doesn't fit on your monitor, you can scroll within the page to display its other contents. If you want to view your page in its entirety, or if you'd like to view the page in more detail, you can change the page's zoom level.

A page's zoom level refers to the magnification OneNote applies to your view of the page. Just as a magnifying glass makes objects appear larger, increasing a page's zoom level makes the page contents that are displayed on the screen appear larger, and decreasing the zoom level makes the contents appear smaller.

6

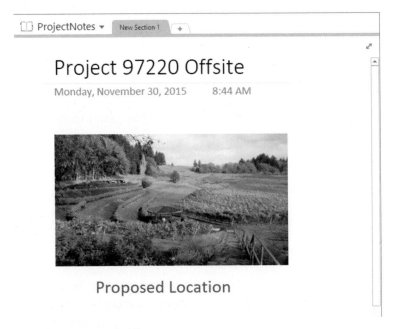

Zoom in to see more detail

Another way to manage the contents of a notebook page is to open a new OneNote window. For example, if you find that you need to switch between areas of the page, and zooming out makes your task more difficult, you can always display your page in a new window. When you display a page in a new window, you create a second copy of the page; any changes you make to either copy also appear in the other window. When you're done editing the page, you can close one window and continue working.

If you want to take notes in a page that takes up part of your screen, you can create a new docked window. A docked window stays attached to a side of the screen, which is the right side by default. You can use a new docked window (next to your existing OneNote window) to take notes on a different page and to create links on one OneNote page to other OneNote pages.

 SEE ALSO For more information about creating linked notes and working with docked windows, see "Manage notebook views and links" earlier in this chapter.

Finally, if you want a notebook window to stay visible on your screen, you can pin it to the top of the open window stack.

To zoom in on a page

1. Do either of the following:

    •   On the **View** tab, in the **Zoom** group, click the **Zoom In** button.

Change the page zoom level to get a new perspective on your notes

    •   Hold down the **Ctrl** key and rotate the mouse wheel forward.

To zoom out on a page

1. Do either of the following:

    •   On the **View** tab, in the **Zoom** group, click the **Zoom Out** button.

    •   Hold down the **Ctrl** key and rotate the mouse wheel backward.

To zoom to 100 percent

1. On the **View** tab, in the **Zoom** group, click the **100%** button.

To zoom to a specific level

1. On the **View** tab, in the **Zoom** group, do either of the following:

    •   Enter a zoom value in the **Zoom** text box.

    •   Click the **Zoom** list arrow, and then click a zoom level.

To zoom so the contents fit in the page width

1. On the **View** tab, in the **Zoom** group, click the **Page Width** button.

To display the current notebook in a new window

1. On the **View** tab, in the **Window** group, click the **New Window** button.

To create a new docked window

1. On the **View** tab, in the **Window** group, click the **New Docked Window** button.

To pin a window to the top of the stack

1. On the **View** tab, in the **Window** group, click the **Always on Top** button.

6

Control page setup

In many cases, taking notes on a blank page with a white background will be the best option for your notebook. The lack of background color and lines provides what is literally a blank slate for you to record your ideas. That said, if you want to change a page's background color, lines, orientation, or size, you can do so quickly. You can also save a set of changes as a template so you can apply it to other pages in your notebook.

OneNote pages have a white background by default. That background works well and provides terrific contrast for the standard colors of ink and most images. If you prefer to create pages with a different background color, perhaps to distinguish pages that contain notes for separate classes or projects, you can select a color from a built-in gallery.

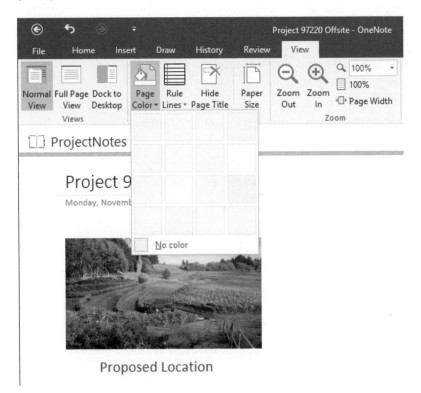

Add color to a page background

Just as you can apply a new background color to a page, you can add, change, or remove background lines. OneNote pages are blank by default, but adding horizontal lines or a grid can help you keep your text notes aligned with the page or can provide a usable background for creating charts and graphs that use ink. Rule lines are a medium gray by default, but you can change that color if you want.

As with documents you might create in Microsoft Word, you can change the size, orientation, and margins of pages in OneNote. Page size is particularly important if you plan to print your notes on paper or in another format, such as a PDF file.

 IMPORTANT When you are creating a custom page size, the width must be between 3 inches and 22 inches and the page's height must be between 1.25 inches and 22 inches.

Page orientation also plays an important part in creating a notebook page. If your page's horizontal and vertical measurements differ, orienting the page so the long edge is on top means that the page is in landscape view, whereas orienting the page so that the short edge is on top means the page is in portrait view.

You can also set your page's margins, which controls the amount of white space between the edge of the page and where the page's contents start. OneNote also comes with a wide variety of page templates that offer standard paper sizes, such as letter size (United States) or A3 (a standard letter size in Europe). If you create a page with settings you want to keep, you can save your settings as a template so that you can easily apply the same settings later.

To set page color

1. On the **View** tab, in the **Page Setup** group, click the **Page Color** button.

2. Click the background color you want to apply to the page.

   Or.

   Click **No Color** to remove a background color from the page.

To set background lines

1. On the **View** tab, in the **Page Setup** group, click the **Rule Lines** button to apply the most recently used line setting.

Or

1. On the **View** tab, click the **Rule Lines** button arrow.

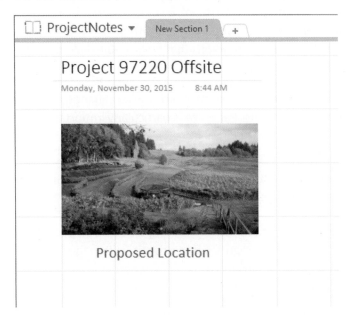

Add background lines to help align your page contents

2. From the gallery that appears, click the line pattern you want to apply.

To change the color of background lines

1. If needed, navigate to a page that has background lines displayed.

2. On the **View** tab, click the **Rule Lines** button arrow, point to **Rule Line Color**, and then click the color you want to apply.

To always create pages with background lines

1. On the **View** tab, click the **Rule Lines** button arrow, and then click **Always Create Pages with Rule Lines**. The pages include the most recently selected line setting.

To remove background lines

1. Navigate to the page that has background lines displayed.

2. On the **View** tab, click the **Rule Lines** button.

   Or

   On the **View** tab, click the **Rule Lines** button arrow, and then click **None**.

To delete the current page title

1. Display the page you want to edit.

2. On the **View** tab, in the **Page Setup** group, click **Hide Page Title**.

3. In the dialog box that appears, click **Yes** to verify that you want to delete the page's title, date, and time.

To apply a built-in page size

1. On the **View** tab, in the **Page Setup** group, click the **Paper Size** button.

2. In the **Paper Size** pane, click the **Size** list arrow, and then click the page size you want to apply.

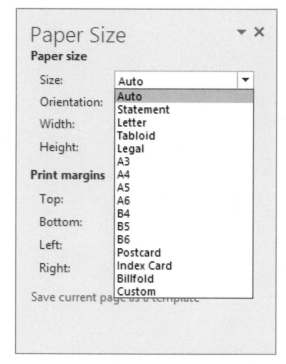

Resize your page by using a variety of built-in paper sizes

To control page orientation

1. On the **View** tab, click **Paper Size**.

2. In the **Paper Size** pane, click the **Size** list arrow, and then click **Custom**.

3. Click the **Orientation** list arrow, and then click either **Portrait** or **Landscape**.

To set a custom page height and width

1. On the **View** tab, click **Paper Size**.

2. In the **Paper Size** pane, click the **Size** list arrow, and then click **Custom**.

3. In the **Paper Size** pane, in the **Width** box, enter the width you want for the page.

4. In the **Height** box, enter the height you want for the page.

To set page print margins

1. On the **View** tab, click **Paper Size**.

2. In the **Paper Size** pane, click the **Size** list arrow, and then click **Custom**.

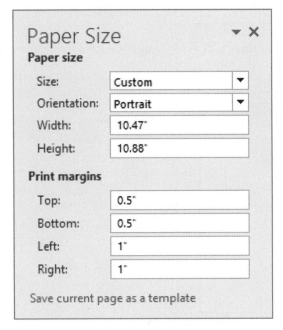

Create custom margins for your notebook page

3. In the **Paper Size** pane, in the **Top** box, enter the size of the top margin.

4. In the **Bottom** box, enter the size of the bottom margin.

5. In the **Left** box, enter the size of the left margin.

6. In the **Right** box, enter the size of the right margin.

To change the paper size units of measurement

1. Click the **File** tab to display the Backstage view, and then click **Options** in the left pane to open the OneNote Options dialog box.

2. In the **OneNote Options** dialog box, click **Advanced**.

3. On the **Advanced** page, scroll down to the **Other** section at the bottom.

4. Click the **Measurement units** list, and select **Inches**, **Centimeters**, **Millimeters**, **Points**, or **Picas**.

5. Click **OK** to save your changes.

To create a paper size template

1. On the **View** tab, click **Paper Size**.

2. In the **Paper Size** pane, set the size, orientation, page dimensions, and margins for the paper size.

3. Click **Save current page as a template**.

4. In the **Save As Template** dialog box, in the **Template name** box, enter a name for your template.

5. Click **Save**.

To apply a custom template

1. On the **Insert** tab of the ribbon, in the **Pages** group, click the **Page Templates** button.

2. In the **Templates** pane, click the **My Templates** header.

 TIP The My Templates header appears at the top of the headers after you have saved a page template.

3. Click the template you want to apply.

Review notes by author and read status

OneNote provides excellent tools to help you collaborate with your colleagues. When you develop a notebook as part of a team, you can have multiple individuals work on the same file. You can then look over the notes by author, identify which notes have not been read, and mark an entire notebook as read. You can also mark a page as read or unread, view which authors made which changes, and display all changes by a specific author or, if you prefer, hide all author information on the page.

As your notebooks change over time, you might want to view your changes by date. For example, you could highlight only those changes made within the past day, two days, a week, or some other time period. To get an idea of the sequence in which changes were made, you can display all of the page's changes sorted by date.

To view the next page that contains unread notes

1. On the **History** tab of the ribbon, in the **Unread** group, click the **Next Unread** button.

    TIP If there are no remaining unread pages in the notebook, the Next Unread button will not be available.

To mark a page as unread

1. Display the notebook page you want to mark as unread.

2. On the **History** tab, in the **Unread** group, click the **Mark as Read** button, and then, in the list, click **Mark as Unread**.

   Or

   Press **Ctrl+Q**.

To mark an entire notebook as read

1. On the **History** tab, in the **Unread** group, click **Mark as Read**, and then, in the list, click **Mark Notebook as Read**.

To show or hide the read status of notebook changes

1. On the **History** tab, click **Mark as Read**, and then click **Show Unread Changes in This Notebook**.

TIP A check mark next to the option means that it is active; clicking the option when it is active removes the check mark and deactivates the option.

To display recent changes

1. On the **History** tab, in the **Authors** group, click **Recent Edits**, and then click the time period you want to apply.

To display changes sorted by date

1. On the **History** tab, in the **Authors** group, click **Recent Edits**, and then click **All Pages Sorted by Date**.

2. If necessary, in the **Search Results** pane, click a header to display the changes within that time period.

To display changes by author

1. On the **History** tab, in the **Authors** group, click **Find by Author**.

2. In the **Search Results** pane, click a header to display the changes made by a specific author.

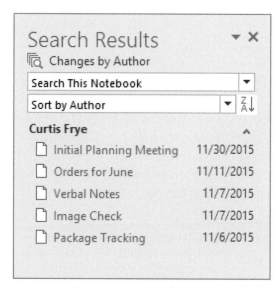

Display changes by author to track notebook use

To show or hide author information on the page

1. On the **History** tab, in the **Authors** group, click **Hide Authors**.

Manage page versions and history

Notebook pages rarely remain static for very long, especially when you use them to keep notes on a class or an ongoing project. OneNote maintains a record of your page's versions, capturing snapshots of the page over time. Each of those page versions is available to you, so if you delete an item but know it was available up to a certain date, you can look through the page's versions to find the item you want.

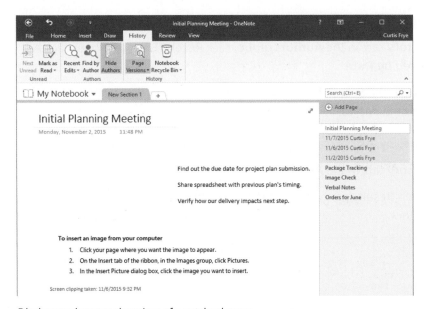

Display previous saved versions of a notebook page

If you don't want to keep past versions of a page, you can always get rid of them. You can also turn off page versioning to stop OneNote from keeping page versions, but doing so prevents you from recovering items you have deleted. If you delete a page, OneNote moves it to the Notebook Recycle Bin. You can restore a page you deleted while it's still in the Notebook Recycle Bin, or you can clear all deleted pages.

 IMPORTANT Clearing the contents of the Notebook Recycle Bin prevents you from restoring a deleted page, so be sure you want to permanently remove its contents.

To display a specific page version

1. On the **History** tab, in the **History** group, click **Page Versions**.

2. In the page tab pane on the right, click the version you want to display.

To delete versions

1. On the **History** tab, in the **History** group, click the **Page Versions** arrow.

2. Click any of the following options:

   - **Delete All Versions in Section**

   - **Delete All Versions in Section Group**

   - **Delete All Versions in Notebook**

To turn the saving of versions on or off for a notebook

1. On the **History** tab, in the **History** group, click the **Page Versions** arrow, and then click **Disable History for this Notebook**.

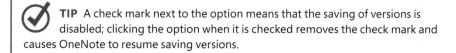

> **TIP** A check mark next to the option means that the saving of versions is disabled; clicking the option when it is checked removes the check mark and causes OneNote to resume saving versions.

2. If a warning dialog box appears, and you want to delete the notebook history and empty the recycle bin, click **Yes**.

To restore a page or section from the Notebook Recycle Bin

1. On the **History** tab, in the **History** group, click the **Notebook Recycle Bin** button.

2. Right-click the tab of the page or section to restore it.

To empty the Notebook Recycle Bin

1. On the **History** tab, in the **History** group, click the **Notebook Recycle Bin** arrow, and then click **Empty Recycle Bin**.

Skills review

In this chapter, you learned how to:

- Manage notebook views and links
- Extend your view by zooming and adding windows
- Control page setup
- Review notes by author and read status
- Manage page versions and history

Practice tasks

The practice files for these tasks are located in the OneNoteSBS\Ch06 folder. The results of the tasks will be automatically saved into the same file in the same folder.

Manage notebook views and links

Open the ManageViews section in OneNote, and then perform the following tasks:

1. Display the notebook in Full Page view.

2. Change the notebook view back to Normal view.

3. Open the **LevelDescriptions** Word document from the practice file folder.

4. Dock the notebook to the desktop, and then create a linked note to the Word file.

Extend your view by zooming and adding windows

Open the AdjustZoom section in OneNote, and then perform the following tasks:

1. Zoom in on the page so the picture appears about twice as large as it is at the 100% zoom level.

2. View the notebook page in a new window, and add a note with the text **Review overall process flow** in the new window.

3. Close the new window.

4. Change the zoom level to **100%**.

Control page setup

Open the ControlPageSetup section in OneNote, and then perform the following tasks:

1. Change the page size to **Tabloid**.

2. Edit the margins so they are all **0.5"**.

3. Change the page's background color to a light blue.

4. Add a wide grid as a background for the page.

Review notes by author and read status

Open the ReviewNotes section in OneNote, and then perform the following tasks:

1. Search to display notes by author.

2. Unhide the authors to see who added which lines.

Manage page versions and history

Open the ManageVersions section in OneNote, and then perform the following tasks:

1. View the notebook page's version history.

2. View the version from November 30, 2015.

3. Switch back to the current version of the page, and then add an item to the High Priority list to see the new version appear in the page tab pane on the right.

Organize notes by using tags and categories

When you take notes in OneNote, you capture important thoughts and action items that will help you in school, at work, or at home. Those notes could include action items you need to complete by your next meeting, ideas for blog posts, or questions you'd like to ask your team leader to get information you need to move forward on a project.

In OneNote, you can add tags to your notebook's contents, identifying categories of information, adding items to your personal to-do list, and summarizing the tags you've created so you have an overview of your ideas and responsibilities going forward.

This chapter guides you through procedures related to adding and removing tags, creating and modifying tags, searching by tag, and summarizing tagged notes.

In this chapter

- Add and remove tags
- Create and modify tags
- Search by tag
- Summarize tagged notes

Practice files

For this chapter, use the practice files from the OneNoteSBS\Ch07 folder. For practice file download instructions, see the introduction.

Add and remove tags

OneNote notebooks are collections of ideas you gather from meetings, presentations, and research. Some of the notes you take will be well organized, following the formal structure of a lecture or the contents of a book. Other notes will be less well structured, representing your own thoughts on a topic, ideas generated during a brainstorming session, or contact information for new colleagues.

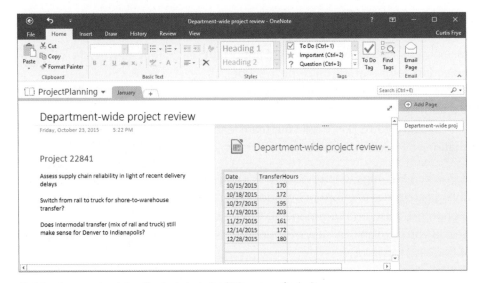

Notebooks organize data effectively but give little sense of priority

Notes provide valuable information about your projects, classes, or whatever you are focusing on. Adding a tag to a note can identify the type of information the note contains, which project it is related to, and whether it represents an action item you have to complete.

OneNote provides many built-in tags; those most commonly used have been assigned keyboard shortcuts. The following table summarizes the types of tags you can create in OneNote by using a keyboard shortcut.

Tag name	Description	Keyboard shortcut
To Do	Assign a task	Ctrl+1
Important	Mark as important	Ctrl+2
Question	Mark as a question to be asked	Ctrl+3

Tag name	Description	Keyboard shortcut
Remember for later	Mark as an item to recall and highlight in yellow	Ctrl+4
Definition	Identify as a definition and highlight in green	Ctrl+5
Highlight	Identify as an item to be highlighted	Ctrl+6
Contact	Identify as contact information	Ctrl+7
Address	Identify as an address	Ctrl+8
Phone number	Identify as a phone number	Ctrl+9

 TIP The To Do tag and its variations have check boxes you can either check or clear to indicate the status of the action item.

7

OneNote also includes tags with which you can identify categories of information useful to your writing, research, and inspiration. Much of the information you tag will relate to your writing and online activities, whether those ideas come from a website or an article, but other notes could provide leads to books, movies, or music that seem interesting to you.

Tag name	Description
Web site to visit	Identify as a website of interest
Idea	Mark as an idea to explore
Password	Identify as a password
Critical	Mark as extremely important information
Movie to see	List a movie of interest
Book to read	List a book of interest
Music to listen to	List a song, album, or artist of interest
Source for article	List as a bibliographic reference
Remember for blog	Identify as an idea for a blog post

IMPORTANT It's not a good security practice to keep passwords in unprotected documents. If you do write down a password in OneNote, be sure to memorize it, or save it in a secure manner, and then erase it from your notebook.

Finally, OneNote comes with a series of tags related to project communication and delivery. You can use these tags to identify topics you should discuss with your colleagues or manager; link information with a project, recommend follow-up in person, by email, or by phone; and prioritize your action items.

Tag name	Description
Discuss with <Person A>	Identify an issue to be discussed with a specific person
Discuss with <Person B>	Identify an issue to be discussed with another person
Discuss with manager	Identify an issue to be discussed with your manager
Project A	Mark information as related to a project
Project B	Mark information as related to another project
Send in email	Tag a request to email information to a colleague
Schedule meeting	Tag a reminder to schedule a meeting
Call back	Tag a request to call back a colleague
To Do priority 1	Identify a high-priority to-do item
To Do priority 2	Identify a lower-priority to-do item
Client request	Mark an action item as a client request

You can add a tag to a line within an existing note or by itself on a note page. Adding a tag to a note or object displays the tag within the body of the object, in the left margin next to the tagged line or object, whereas adding a tag by itself on a note page creates a new note in which you can type text associated with the tag.

 TIP You can add multiple tags to the same object.

Friday, October 23, 2015   5:22 PM

Project 22841

Assess supply chain reliability in light of recent delivery delays

Switch from rail to truck for shore-to-warehouse transfer?

Does intermodal transfer (mix of rail and truck) still make sense for Denver to Indianapolis?

Adding a tag by itself creates a text box for you to enter a note on your topic

As with other objects within a OneNote notebook, it's likely that you will need to delete tags when they no longer contribute to your work. Removing a tag is also a straightforward process—all you need to do is identify the tag and tell OneNote to get rid of it. If you delete a tag you added by itself, rather than as an addition to an existing note, the text box that OneNote created along with the tag will be removed from your notebook, but your cursor remains in place so that you can begin a note.

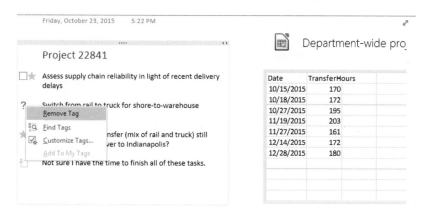

Right-click a tag to remove it from your notebook

To add a tag to an existing note

1. Click within the line of text to which you want to add a tag.

2. On the **Home** tab of the ribbon, in the **Tags** group, click the **More** arrow in the lower-right corner of the **Tags** gallery.

> **TIP** If you docked OneNote or resized the window, the Tags gallery is condensed into the Tag button. Instead of the More arrow, click the Tag button.

3. Click the tag you want to add.

Or

1. Right-click the note to which you want to add a tag.

2. On the **Mini Toolbar**, click the **Tag** button's arrow, and then click the tag you want to add.

To add a tag to a page

1. Click the spot on the page where you want to add a tag.

2. On the **Home** tab, in the **Tags** group, click the **More** arrow in the lower-right corner of the **Tags** gallery.

3. Click the tag you want to add.

4. Add text to the text box that OneNote created along with the tag.

Or

1. Right-click the spot on the page where you want to add a tag.

2. On the **Mini Toolbar**, click the **Tag** button's arrow, and then click the tag you want to add.

3. Add text to the text box that OneNote created along with the tag.

To add a To Do tag

1. Do either of the following:

    *   Click the note to which you want to add the To Do tag.

    *   Click a blank spot on the active page.

2. Do either of the following:

    *   On the **Home** tab, in the **Tags** group, click the **To Do Tag** button.

    *   Press **Ctrl+1**.

Or

1. Do either of the following:

    *   Right-click the note to which you want to add the To Do tag.

    *   Right-click a blank spot on the active page.

2. On the **Mini Toolbar**, click the **Tag as To Do** button.

To remove a tag

1. Click anywhere in the line of text that has the tag.

2. On the **Home** tab, in the **Tags** group, click the **More** arrow in the lower-right corner of the **Tags** gallery.

3. At the bottom of the gallery, click **Remove Tag**.

 TIP The Remove Tag button in the ribbon and on the Mini Toolbar removes all the tags associated with that line of text.

Or

1. Right-click the note whose tag you want to remove.

2. On the **Mini Toolbar**, click the **Tag** arrow, and then click **Remove Tag** at the bottom of the gallery.

Or

1. Do either of the following:

    *   Right-click the tag, and then click **Remove Tag**.

    *   With your cursor to the immediate right of the tag, press **Backspace**.

Create and modify tags

OneNote includes quite a few built-in tags, but they're meant for general use and might not be the best choice in all circumstances. For example, you could keep notes about several different projects in your notebook. Creating a tag for each of those projects will make it easier to locate information as your notebook's contents grow.

Creating a new tag requires you to give your tag a name, symbol, font color, and highlight color. OneNote displays a preview of your settings in the New Tag dialog box, so you'll have a good idea of what your tag will look like when you add it to your notebook.

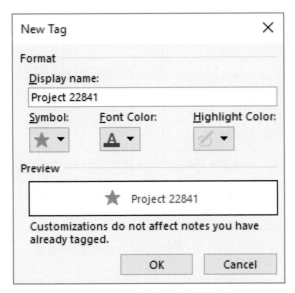

Create a custom tag using the New Tag dialog box

 TIP Tags you create appear at the top of the Tags gallery.

Modifying an existing tag is similar to creating a custom tag. Rather than defining a new tag, you identify the tag you want to modify and make your changes. The dialog box is the same one you use for creating a new tag—only the name is different.

Modifying a tag changes the characteristics of tags you apply from that point on, but it doesn't change tags of that type that you have already added to your notebook.

> **TIP** In most apps, you can add custom tags, but you can't modify existing tags. OneNote lets you modify all tags. If you're going to change a tag significantly, it's better to create a custom tag than to modify an existing one.

To create a custom tag

1. On the **Home** tab, in the **Tags** group, click the **More** arrow in the lower-right corner of the **Tags** gallery.

2. At the bottom of the gallery, click **Customize Tags**.

3. In the **Customize Tags** dialog box, click the **New Tag** button.

4. In the **New Tag** dialog box, in the **Display name** box, enter a name for your tag.

5. Do any of the following:

   • Click the **Symbol** button, and then select a symbol from the gallery that appears.

   • Click the **Font Color** arrow, and then select a color from the palette.

   • Click the **Highlight Color** button, and then select a highlight color from the palette.

6. Click **OK**. The new custom tag appears at the top of the All Tags gallery in the Customize Tags dialog box.

7. In the **Customize Tags** dialog box, click **OK**.

To modify an existing tag

1. On the **Home** tab, in the **Tags** group, click the **More** arrow in the lower-right corner of the **Tags** gallery.

2. At the bottom of the gallery list, click **Customize Tags**.

3. In the **Customize Tags** dialog box, in the **All Tags** list, click the tag you want to modify.

7

4. Click the **Modify Tag** button.

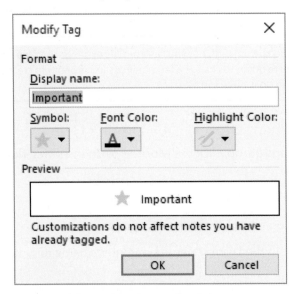

Use the Modify Tag dialog box to edit existing tags

5. In the **Modify Tag** dialog box, do any of the following:

   - In the **Display name** box, enter a new name for your tag.

   - Click the **Symbol** button, and then select a new symbol from the gallery.

   - Click the **Font Color** button, and then select a new color from the palette.

   - Click the **Highlight Color** button, and then select a new highlight color from the palette.

6. Click **OK**.

7. In the **Customize Tags** dialog box, click **OK**.

Search by tag

Tags provide useful visual indicators within your notebooks, but they also give OneNote information it can use to help you find the notes you need to complete your projects. OneNote displays the results of your search in the Tags Summary pane, which organizes the tagged notes according to the grouping you select.

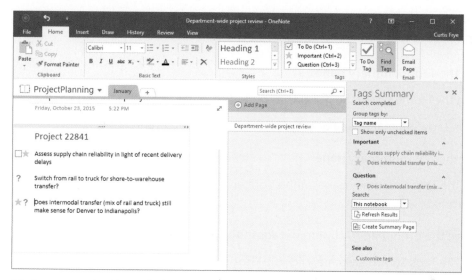

Display your notebook's tags in the Tags Summary pane

You can choose to group your tags by tag name, the section the notes appear in, the text of the notes themselves (in ascending alphabetical order), or other groupings. If you think your notebook might contain action items that you've missed, or at least haven't completed yet, you can show unchecked items only.

> ⚠ **IMPORTANT** When you display unchecked items only, OneNote limits its display to tags with a check box. Tags such as Important or Question, which don't have check boxes associated with them, don't appear in the summary.

By default, searches look within the active notebook. If you want, you can change the scope of the search to include specific groups, sections, or pages; expand the search to include other notebooks; or limit your search by time, displaying just those notes recorded today, yesterday, last week, or any notes recorded more than a week ago. Whenever you change the search's scope, you can refresh your results to see the outcome of your changes.

When you're done working with the Tags Summary pane, you can close it and return the display space to the notebook's contents.

To open the Tags Summary pane

1. On the **Home** tab of the ribbon, in the **Tags** group, click the **Find Tags** button.

   The Tags Summary pane displays all the tags in the current scope.

To close the Tags Summary pane

1. In the **Tags Summary** pane, at the right end of the title bar, click the **Close** button.

To change the order and grouping of tags in the Tags Summary pane

1. In the **Tags Summary** pane, click the **Group tags by** arrow in the list box.

2. Click the grouping scheme you want to apply.

To hide a specific group of tags

1. If necessary, open the **Tags Summary** pane.

2. In the **Tags Summary** pane, click the hide detail button (the upward-pointing caret) next to the title of the group you want to hide.

To display a specific group of tags

1. If necessary, open the **Tags Summary** pane.

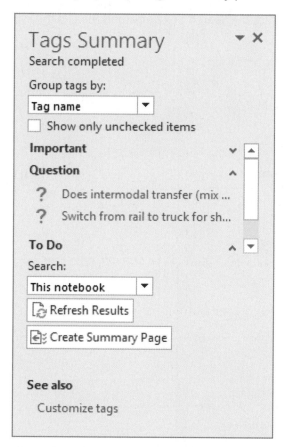

Show or hide tag categories in the Tags Summary pane

2. In the **Tags Summary** pane, click the show detail button (the downward-pointing caret) next to the title of the group you want to display.

To display unchecked items only

1. If necessary, open the **Tags Summary** pane.

2. In the **Tags Summary** pane, select the **Show only unchecked items** check box.

To change the scope of your search

1. If necessary, open the **Tags Summary** pane.

2. In the **Tags Summary** pane, click the **Search** box arrow and then, in the list, click the scope you want to apply.

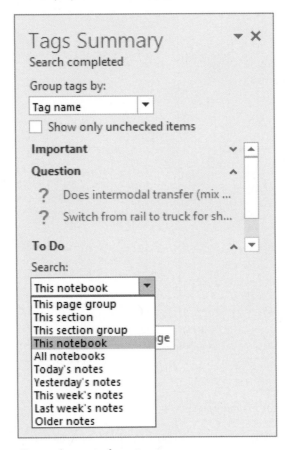

Change the scope of your tag summary

3. If necessary, click **Refresh Results**.

Summarize tagged notes

As you add content to your OneNote notebooks, you'll find that the tags you add to your notes will start to blend in, especially if you add images or shapes. You can ensure that you haven't missed any important information by summarizing all of your tagged notes onto a new page.

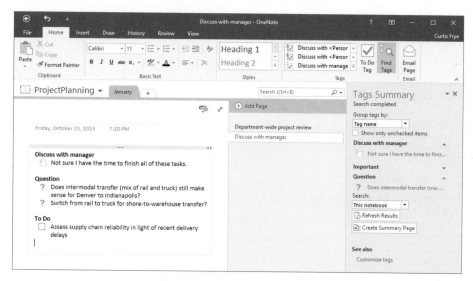

Create a new notebook page to summarize your notebook's tags

The summary page displays the contents of the Tags Summary pane, so the filters and organization you've set will be reflected on the new page. The summary page's name will be the same as the first category of tags displayed in summary.

> **IMPORTANT** Notes on the summary page are copies of the original notes, but they aren't linked to the originals. If you clear or check a To Do tag's check box on the summary page, that change won't affect the original note (and vice versa).

In notebooks that contain more than one or two pages, it's likely you won't remember exactly where a note came from within that notebook. While you are on the summary page, you can point to a note, or click or tap the note, to display an indicator next to the tag. Clicking or tapping the indicator will take you to the original note so you can see it in its original context.

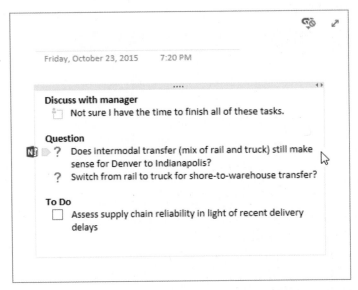

Click the indicator (OneNote icon) next to a note on a summary page to view the original note

Creating a tag summary page lists every tag displayed in the Tags Summary pane, including any tags on an existing tag summary page. In other words, if your notebook already contains a tag summary page, creating a new summary will also list those tags, so many will be duplicated. To avoid this problem, delete any existing summary pages before creating a new one.

OneNote creates the summary page; it is a best practice to change the page's title to indicate that it is a summary. For example, you might change the title from *To Do List* to *SUMMARY: All Analytics Projects*.

To create a tag summary page

1. If necessary, on the **Home** tab of the ribbon, click the **Find Tags** button to open the **Tags Summary** pane.

2. Click the **Create summary page** button.

3. At the top of the new tags summary page, enter a title in the title area.

To view a summarized note in its original context

1. Display the summary page in your notebook.

2. With your mouse, point to the note you want to investigate.

3. Click the **OneNote** icon that appears next to the note.

Skills review

7

In this chapter, you learned how to:

- Add and remove tags
- Create and modify tags
- Search by tag
- Summarize tagged notes

Practice tasks

The practice files for these tasks are located in the OneNoteSBS\Ch07 folder. The results of the tasks will be automatically saved into the same file in the same folder.

Add and remove tags

Open the AddTags section in OneNote, and then perform the following tasks:

1. Add a **To Do** tag to each of the first three items in the list.

2. Check one of the notes as having been completed.

3. Add an **Important** tag to one of the notes not marked as completed.

4. Mark the final note as a question.

5. Remove a note and its tag from the list.

Create and modify tags

Open the CreateTags section in OneNote, and then perform the following tasks:

1. Define a new tag named **Project 22841**, with a custom icon and font color.

2. Tag two notes by using the **Project 22841** tag.

3. Modify the **Project 22841** tag so it has a distinct highlighting color.

4. Tag a different note with the new version of the tag.

Search by tag

Open the SearchByTags section in OneNote, and then perform the following tasks:

1. List all of the tags in your notebook.

2. Hide the notes within the **To Do** and **Question** categories.

 TIP Use the Group Tags By list box to switch the type of grouping.

3. Display only the notes within the **To Do** category.

4. Group the tags by note text.

Summarize tagged notes

Open the SummarizeTags section in OneNote, and then perform the following tasks:

1. Create a summary page from the notes in your notebook.

2. Rename the summary page to **Note Summary**.

3. Point to a note and click the **OneNote** indicator that appears, to view the note on its original page.

Print and share notebooks and pages

OneNote is a terrific app for capturing and managing your notes, but it works best when you use it to collaborate with other users. One great way to collaborate is to print a paper copy of a notebook, section, or page. Although a paper copy of a file isn't as versatile as an electronic copy, it captures the file at a moment in time and provides a reference for discussions.

You can also share notebooks and portions of notebooks by exporting the files to other electronic formats, using the files as the basis for email attachments, and uploading the files to Microsoft OneDrive accounts. On OneDrive, you can share the files through a variety of methods while retaining control over whether your colleagues can edit the files or just view them. Microsoft SharePoint provides similar capabilities as OneDrive and is available to many enterprise customers.

This chapter guides you through procedures related to previewing and printing notebook content; exporting pages, sections, and notebooks; sending pages to colleagues; and sharing notebooks by using OneDrive and SharePoint.

In this chapter

- Preview and print notebook content
- Export pages, sections, and notebooks
- Send pages to colleagues
- Share notebooks by using OneDrive
- Share notebooks by using SharePoint

Practice files

For this chapter, use the practice files from the OneNoteSBS\Ch08 folder. For practice file download instructions, see the introduction.

Preview and print notebook content

OneNote provides outstanding tools for maintaining your notebooks in digital form, whether you keep your notes on your personal computer, laptop, tablet, phone, or on OneDrive. While your notes remain in a OneNote notebook, you can add to the file and edit its contents. You can also print a notebook page to create a paper copy of the page's current state. If you want to see what your page will look like when printed, you can preview the page within OneNote.

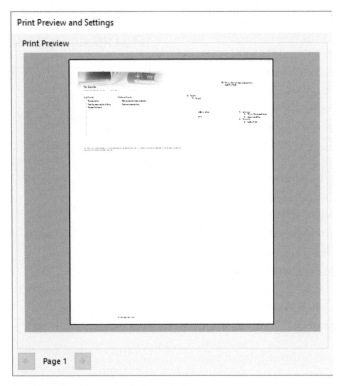

Preview a OneNote page before printing

While in Print Preview, you can change the page's paper size, scaling, orientation, and footer contents (which appear at the bottom of each printed page). Changing these aspects of your page only affects the preview and the printout—the underlying characteristics of your page won't change.

 SEE ALSO For information about changing paper size, orientation, and other characteristics, see "Control page setup" in Chapter 6, "Manage views, windows, and page versions."

When you display a page in Print Preview, you might find that the page will print on more than one page of paper. If that's the case, you can move through the preview one page at a time to see how your page will appear when printed. When you are satisfied with the preview, you can print your page to any available printer.

 SEE ALSO For information about saving a page, section, or notebook as a PDF or XPS file, see "Export pages, sections, and notebooks" later in this chapter.

To preview a notebook page before printing it

1. Display the page you want to preview.

2. Click the **File** tab of the ribbon to display the Backstage view.

3. In the Backstage view, click **Print**.

4. On the **Print** page of the Backstage view, click **Print Preview** to open the Print Preview And Settings dialog box.

    The notebook page is displayed in the Print Preview section of the dialog box.

To change the print settings of a notebook page

1. Open the **Print Preview and Settings** dialog box for the page whose print settings you want to change.

2. Use the tools in the **Print Settings** section of the dialog box to change the following settings:

    • Print Range, which determines whether to print the current page (the default), page group, or current section.

    • Paper Size, which selects the physical size of the paper to be printed on. This size can be a built-in specification, such as U.S. Letter, or a custom size defined by the user.

    • Scaling, which you specify by selecting or clearing the Scale Content To Paper Width check box. If the check box is selected, OneNote changes the size of the OneNote document's contents so they fit on the selected page size based on the page's width.

8

- Orientation, which specifies whether to turn the page so the short edge is on top (portrait orientation) or the long edge is on top (landscape orientation).

- Footer, which can include combinations of the section name and page number or can be blank. If you select the Start Page Numbering At 1 check box, the printed pages will be printed with page numbers starting at 1, regardless of their actual number within the section.

Define print settings to control how your page will appear when printed

To page through a print preview

1. Open the **Print Preview and Settings** dialog box for the page whose print preview you want to view.

2. If you have more than one page, in the lower-left corner of the **Print Preview and Settings** dialog box, do either of the following:

   - Click the **Next Page** button to view the next page of the preview.

   - Click the **Previous Page** button to view the previous page of the preview.

To print all or part of a notebook from the Print Preview And Settings dialog box

1. Open the **Print Preview and Settings** dialog box for the page you want to print.

2. Use the tools in the **Print Settings** section of the dialog box to change the print settings until the page displayed in the preview window looks the way you want your printout to look.

3. Click the **Print** button.

4. In the **Print** dialog box, if necessary, change the following settings:

   - **Select Printer**

   - **Page Range**

   - **Number of copies**

5. Click the **Print** button.

To quickly print a notebook page

1. With the page you want to print displayed, click the **File** tab of the ribbon to display the Backstage view, and then click **Print**.

2. On the **Print** page of the Backstage view, click **Print**.

3. In the **Print** dialog box, if necessary, change the following settings:

   - **Select Printer**

   - **Page Range**

   - **Number of copies**

4. Click the **Print** button.

8

Export pages, sections, and notebooks

OneNote gives you a lot of flexibility in working with your files, including the ability to export your files to other formats. Common formats for exchanging documents include the PDF and the Microsoft XML Paper Specification (XPS) formats. Files in PDF and XPS formats can be exchanged easily and opened by using free reader software. You can also export files as OneNote sections, Microsoft Word documents, and single-file webpages.

Select a target format for a file you export from OneNote

To export the current page

1. Display the page you want to export.

2. Display the **Export** page of the Backstage view. In the **Export Current** area, click **Page**.

3. In the **File Types** list, click the format to which you want to export the page.

4. Click **Export**.

5. In the **Save As** dialog box, navigate to the folder where you want to save the exported page.

6. In the **File name** box, enter a name for the exported page.

7. Click **Save**.

> **TIP** If you change your mind and decide you want to export the current section or notebook, select the appropriate option at the bottom of the Save As dialog box. Or, if you want to change the file format, click the Save As Type list and then click a file type.

To export the current section

1. Display a page in the section you want to export.

2. Display the **Export** page of the Backstage view. In the **Export Current** area, click **Section**.

3. In the **File Types** list, click the format to which you want to export the section.

4. Click **Export**.

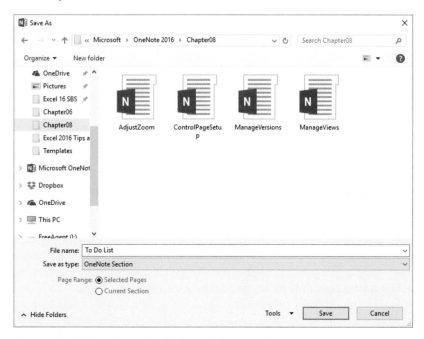

Export a OneNote section to the file format of your choice

5. In the **Save As** dialog box, navigate to the folder where you want to save the exported section.

6. In the **File name** box, enter a name for the exported section.

7. Click **Save**.

To export selected pages from a section

1. Display the section from which you want to export selected pages.

2. In the page tab pane at the right side of the active page, click the first page you want to export and then, while holding down the **Ctrl** key, click the tabs of the other pages you want to export.

3. Display the **Export** page of the Backstage view.

4. In the **Export Current** area, click **Section**.

5. Click **Export**.

6. In the **Save As** dialog box, in the **Page Range** area, select **Selected Pages**.

7. Navigate to the folder where you want to save the exported pages.

8. In the **File name** box, enter a name for the exported file.

9. Click **Save**.

To export the current notebook

1. Display a page in the notebook you want to export.

2. If necessary, on the **Export** page of the Backstage view, in the **Export Current** area, click **Notebook**.

3. In the **File Types** list, click the format to which you want to export the notebook.

4. Click **Export**.

5. In the **Save As** dialog box, navigate to the folder where you want to save the exported notebook.

6. In the **File name** box, enter a name for the exported notebook.

7. Click **Save**.

Send pages to colleagues

OneNote enhances your ability to share your work with your colleagues in several ways. For example, you can embed a OneNote page in the body of an email message. Depending on your email program's settings, the appearance of the page might change, but the contents will arrive in your colleague's inbox. If your colleagues prefer to receive the page as a OneNote file attached to an email message, or as a PDF attachment, you can send it that way, too. When you send the page as a OneNote file, you also send an .mht attachment, which your recipient can open to view the content as a webpage.

Word users can also take advantage of the collaboration capabilities built into OneNote by sending pages to Word documents that can be edited in Word and then shared.

To send a page in the body of an email message

1. Display the page you want to send.

2. Click the **File** tab and then, in the Backstage view, click **Send**.

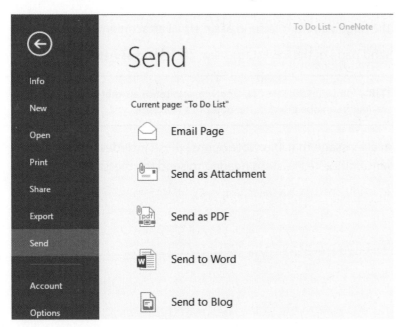

Use the Send page of the Backstage view to share your OneNote files

3. On the **Send** page of the Backstage view, click **Email Page**.

4. In the email message that OneNote opens, which includes the contents of the page, add the email address of the recipient and any other information you want, and then send the message as usual.

Or

1. Display the page you want to send.

2. On the **Home** tab, in the **Email** group, click **Email Page**.

3. In the email message that opens, add any recipients and other information, and then send the message.

> ⚠ **IMPORTANT** To share a OneNote page directly in email, you must have Outlook 2013 or later installed. The feature isn't available on Windows RT. The option will still be there, but it might not generate an email message. To share notes attached to an email, you can use Outlook or an email service such as Outlook.com or Hotmail.

To send a page as an email attachment

1. Display the page you want to send as an email attachment.

2. On the **Send** page of the Backstage view, click **Send as Attachment**.

> **TIP** Along with the .one file, OneNote also sends an .mht file, which your recipient can open to view the notes as a webpage.

3. In the email message that OneNote opens, which includes the page as an attachment, complete the steps needed to send the message.

To send a page as a PDF email attachment

1. Display the page you want to send as a PDF file.

2. On the **Send** page of the Backstage view, click **Send as PDF**.

3. In the email message that OneNote opens, which includes a PDF rendering of the page as an attachment, complete the steps needed to send the message.

To send a page as a Word document

> **IMPORTANT** You must have Word installed to perform this procedure.

1. Display the page you want to send to a Word file.

2. On the **Send** page of the Backstage view, click **Send to Word**. OneNote opens the page as a Word document.

3. Edit the Word document as you want. You can then share the Word document with your colleagues by attaching it to an email, uploading it to a SharePoint site, or using another method.

> **TIP** You can also create a new OneNote page by sending an email to OneNote. Start by sending an email to *me@onenote.com*. You will receive an email reply that contains setup instructions. You can add all your email addresses to your Microsoft account, as aliases. After you specify a notebook for the email notes, you can instantly create new OneNote pages by sending emails from any of your registered aliases to *me@onenote.com*.

8

Share notebooks by using OneDrive

OneDrive is an online service that provides a useful and accessible means of sharing files with your colleagues. You can create a OneDrive account, which comes with enough storage space for most users, for free. After you establish your account, you can upload files from your computer, create notebooks by using Office Online, and download files from OneDrive to your computer.

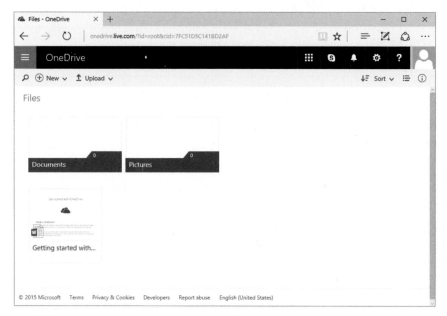

Establish a OneDrive account to save and share files over the web

You can navigate within OneDrive by using commands that are very similar to navigating within both File Explorer and SharePoint. After you have stored a notebook in OneDrive, you can share it with your colleagues. You have a wide variety of options for sharing a notebook, including whether to allow your colleagues to edit the file or just view it. You can also choose to share the file by emailing a hyperlink to the file. When you share a file stored in a OneDrive folder, you can specify whether the linked file can be edited or just viewed by individuals who have the file's address.

 TIP If your computer is running Windows 7, use Windows Explorer to navigate your files and folders whenever the text mentions File Explorer.

To create a OneDrive account

1. In your web browser, go to the OneDrive home page at *onedrive.com*.

2. Click **Sign Up**.

3. Click **Create a Microsoft account**.

4. In the email address box, enter the email address you want to associate with the account.

5. In the **Create password** box, enter a password for the account.

6. To opt out of receiving promotional emails, clear the **Send me promotional emails from Microsoft** check box.

7. Click **Next**.

8. Open your email program and the *Verify your email address* email from the Microsoft account team. Click the blue **Verify** box to verify your email address.

9. Click **OK**.

To sign in to OneDrive

1. In your web browser, go to the OneDrive home page.

2. Click **Sign in**.

3. Enter your account name (usually an email address) and press **Enter**.

4. Enter your password and press **Enter**.

To upload a file or folder to OneDrive

1. In OneDrive, click the **Upload** button on the toolbar.

2. Do either of the following:

    *   Click **Files** to upload one or more files.

    *   Click **Folder** to upload a folder.

3. In the **Open** dialog box, select the files or folder you want to upload.

4. Click **Open**.

8

To download a file from OneDrive

1. In a folder that contains at least one file, point to the icon representing the file you want to download, and select the round check box that appears in the upper-right corner of the icon.

2. On the menu bar, click **Download** to download the file to your computer's Downloads folder.

To create a new OneNote notebook on OneDrive

1. Open your OneDrive account in your web browser.

2. Click **New**, and then click **OneNote notebook**.

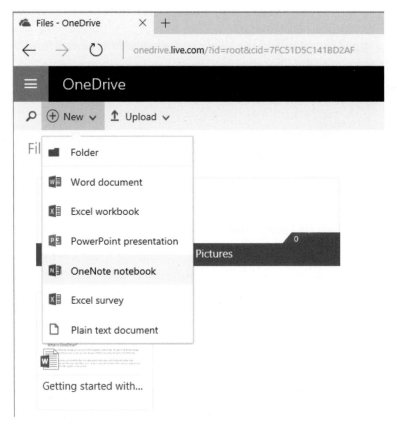

Create a new OneNote notebook in OneNote Online

3. In the dialog box that opens, enter the OneNote notebook name, and then click **Create**. OneNote Online opens.

To open a OneNote notebook stored in OneDrive in the desktop version of OneNote

1. In the desktop version of OneNote, click the **File** tab of the ribbon, and then click **Open** to display the Open page of the Backstage view.

2. In the **Open from OneDrive** section, in the **My Notebooks** panel, double-click the notebook you want to open.

Or

1. In the desktop version of OneNote, display the **Open** page of the Backstage view.

2. At the bottom of the **Open from OneDrive** section, click the **Manage notebooks on OneDrive** link.

3. When your OneDrive directory appears in your web browser, click the OneNote file you want to open. It opens in OneNote Online.

To share an online notebook with your colleagues by using email

1. In OneDrive, open the notebook you want to share.

2. On the title bar of the online notebook (in the upper-middle area of the screen), click **Share** to display the Invite People page of the Share dialog box.

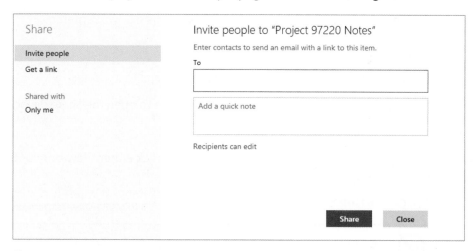

Share a OneNote Online notebook with your colleagues

3. In the **Share** dialog box, enter the email addresses of the colleagues with whom you want to share the notebook.

4. In the **Add a quick note** box, enter a note describing the file to give your colleagues some context for how to work with the file.

5. Click **Recipients can edit** to open two list boxes.

6. In the top list box, do either of the following:

    - Select **Recipients can edit** to allow the people you have invited to make changes to your notebook.

    - Select **Recipients can only view** to restrict access to read-only.

7. In the bottom list box, do either of the following:

    - Select **Recipients don't need a Microsoft account** to allow recipients without Microsoft accounts to access the notebook.

    - Select **Recipients need to sign in with a Microsoft account** to require Microsoft account sign-in.

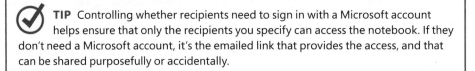 **TIP** Controlling whether recipients need to sign in with a Microsoft account helps ensure that only the recipients you specify can access the notebook. If they don't need a Microsoft account, it's the emailed link that provides the access, and that can be shared purposefully or accidentally.

8. Click **Share**. An invitation is sent to the email addresses you entered.

To create a link to share a notebook from OneDrive

1. In OneDrive, open the notebook you want to share.

2. On the title bar of the online notebook, click **Share** to open the Share dialog box.

3. In the **Share** dialog box, click **Get a link**.

4. Click the **Choose an option** list arrow, and then click either **View only** or **Edit** to set user editing privileges.

5. Click **Create Link**.

 TIP The link that is created is quite long. If you want a shorter link, click Shorten Link.

Create a link to a file you want to share with your colleagues

6. Copy the link to the Clipboard.

7. Do either of the following:

    •   Paste the link into an email message, a webpage, or a document to share the link.

    •   Click one of the social media sharing buttons available under the link box, and follow the instructions to send the link.

8. In the **Share** dialog box, click **Close**.

To add a OneDrive directory to your list of places

1. In the Backstage view, click **Share**.

2. On the **Share** page, click **Add a Place**.

3. In the **Add a Place** list, click **OneDrive**.

4. In the **Add a service** dialog box, enter the email address for the Microsoft account associated with your OneDrive site, and then click **Next**.

5. In the **Sign in** dialog box, in the **Password** field, enter the password for the Microsoft account.

6. Click **Sign in**. OneNote opens the Add Service dialog box that shows its progress in making the connection. When the app establishes the connection, the site appears in the Backstage view.

Share notebooks by using SharePoint

SharePoint provides a platform on which members of an organization can collaborate, communicate, and share files. Regardless of whether you work alone or as part of a team, SharePoint provides tools you can use to organize your files, contacts, and project information.

The full range of capabilities available through SharePoint are beyond the scope of this book. This topic focuses on using SharePoint together with OneNote to share project notebooks with your colleagues. When you open a SharePoint site in your web browser, the interface looks very similar to that of OneDrive.

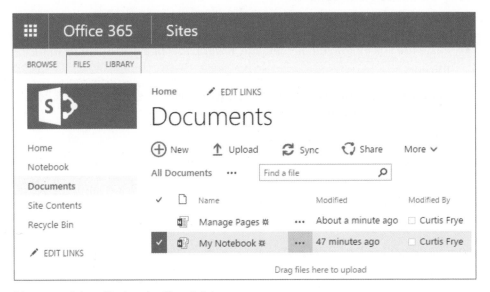

Manage and share files by using SharePoint

You can create a connection to a SharePoint site from within OneNote, and then export files (save copies) to the site for use by your team. After you have the notebook on SharePoint, you can grant access to it by sharing a link through instant messages or email messages, or as a hyperlink in a Word document or other file. You can also move the file from SharePoint to another location from within OneNote.

 TIP Many SharePoint installations include OneDrive accounts, so adding a SharePoint site as a place might also add a OneDrive place.

After you create a notebook on SharePoint or export or move a notebook to SharePoint, you can share the file from within OneNote. As with other sharing methods, you can share with specific colleagues by using email, by getting a sharing link, and by sharing with a meeting that allows OneNote sharing.

> ⚠ **IMPORTANT** A fourth sharing option, Move Notebook, can cause problems with your notebook if you have already shared it. When you click Move Notebook, the app displays a message indicating that moving a shared notebook can cause significant issues, including data loss. For that reason, we recommend not moving a shared notebook.

To add a SharePoint site to your list of places

1. Click the **File** tab of the ribbon to display the Backstage view, and then click **Share**.

2. On the **Share** page, click **Add a Place**.

    > **TIP** Depending on where the active notebook is stored, you might not see the Add A Place option.

3. In the **Add a Place** list, click **Office 365 SharePoint**.

4. In the **Add a service** dialog box, enter the email address associated with your SharePoint site, and then click **Next**.

5. In the **Sign in** dialog box, in the **Password** field, enter the password for the Microsoft account.

6. Click **Sign in**. OneNote opens the Add Service dialog box that shows its progress in making the connection. When the app establishes the connection, the site appears in the Backstage view.

To copy a notebook to SharePoint

1. Use the export procedure provided earlier in this chapter to export a notebook as a OneNote Package (a OneNote notebook saved as a single file).

2. In your web browser, open your SharePoint site.

3. In the navigation bar on the left side of the SharePoint webpage, click the document library in which you want to store the notebook.

4. In Windows, open File Explorer, navigate to the folder that contains the OneNote package, and then drag the package from File Explorer to the document library displayed in your web browser.

Or

8

1. Export a notebook to a OneNote Package.

2. In your web browser, open your SharePoint site.

3. In the navigation bar on the left side of the SharePoint webpage, click **Documents**.

4. On the toolbar of the **Documents** webpage, click **Upload**.

5. In the **Add a Document** dialog box, click **Choose Files**.

6. In the **Choose a File to Upload** dialog box, click the OneNote package you want to upload, and then click **Open**.

7. In the **Add a Document** dialog box, click **OK**.

To share a notebook from SharePoint by using email

1. In SharePoint, click to the left of the notebook you want to share so that a check mark appears beside the file name.

2. On the toolbar of the **Documents** webpage, click **Share**.

3. In the **Share** dialog box, enter the email addresses of the colleagues with whom you want to share the notebook.

> **TIP** After you enter an address, SharePoint will automatically sync and set the email address so that you can delete it or add a new one.

4. In the **Add a quick note** box, enter a note describing the file to give your colleagues some context for how to work with the file.

5. Click **Recipients can edit** to open two list boxes.

6. In the top list box, do either of the following:

    - Select **Recipients can edit** to allow the people you have invited to make changes to your notebook.

    - Select **Recipients can only view** to restrict access to read-only.

7. In the bottom list box, do either of the following:

   - Select **Recipients don't need a Microsoft account** to allow recipients without Microsoft accounts to access the notebook.

   - Select **Recipients need to sign in with a Microsoft account** to require Microsoft account sign-in.

8. Click **Share**. An invitation is sent to the email addresses you entered.

To create a link to share a notebook from SharePoint

1. In SharePoint, click to the left of the notebook you want to share so that a check mark appears beside the file name.

2. On the document library toolbar, click **Share**.

3. In the **Share** dialog box, click **Get a link**.

4. Click the **Choose an option** arrow, and then click either **View only** or **Edit** to set user editing privileges.

5. Click **Create Link**.

6. Copy the link to the Clipboard.

7. Do either of the following:

   - Paste the link into an email message, a webpage, or a document to share the link.

   - Click one of the social media sharing buttons available under the link box, and follow the instructions to send the link.

8. In the **Share** dialog box, click **Close**.

8

To move a notebook to SharePoint from within OneNote

1. Open the notebook that you want to move to SharePoint.

2. Click **Share** in the Backstage view to display the Share page.

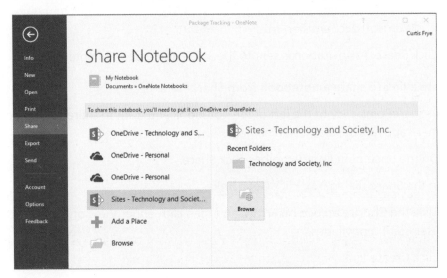

Move a OneNote file to SharePoint to facilitate collaboration

3. Click the SharePoint site to which you want to move the notebook.

4. Click **Browse**.

5. In the **Move Notebook** dialog box, navigate to the folder to which you want to move the notebook.

6. Click **Move**.

To share a notebook saved on SharePoint from within OneNote by using email

1. In the OneNote desktop app, open a notebook that is stored in SharePoint.

2. Display the **Share** page of the Backstage view.

3. Click **Share with People**.

4. In the **Share with People** area, enter the email addresses of the colleagues with whom you want to share the notebook.

5. In the **Include a personal message with the invitation** box, enter a note that describes the file, to give your colleagues some context for how to work with the file.

6. Click the **Can Edit** list arrow, and then do either of the following:

   - Click **Can edit** to allow recipients to edit the file.

   - Click **Can view** to allow recipients to view the file but not edit it.

7. Click **Share**.

To share a notebook saved on SharePoint with a meeting

1. In the OneNote desktop app, open a notebook that is stored in SharePoint.

2. Display the **Share** page of the Backstage view.

3. In the **Share** area, click **Share with Meeting**. Then in the **Share with Meeting** area, click the **Share with Meeting** button.

4. In the **Share Notes with an Online Meeting** dialog box that opens, click the meeting that you want to share the notebook with.

5. Click **OK**.

Skills review

In this chapter, you learned how to:

- Preview and print notebook content

- Export pages, sections, and notebooks

- Send pages to colleagues

- Share notebooks by using OneDrive

- Share notebooks by using SharePoint

Practice tasks

The practice files for these tasks are located in the OneNoteSBS\Ch08 folder. The results of the tasks will be automatically saved into the same file in the same folder.

Preview and print notebook content

Open the PrintNotebooks section in OneNote, and then perform the following tasks:

1. Display the section's page in **Print Preview**, and then change the paper size to **A5**.

2. Clear the **Scale content to paper width** check box, and display the second page of the preview.

3. Select the **Scale content to paper width** check box, and change the paper size back to **Letter**.

4. Edit the footer so it displays only the page number.

5. Click **Print**, and then print the page on your printer.

Export pages, sections, and notebooks

 IMPORTANT You must have Word installed in order to perform this set of tasks.

Open the ExportPages section in OneNote, and then perform the following tasks:

1. Export the section's page to a Word document.

2. Export the page to a PDF file.

3. View both the Word and PDF files and compare the differences.

Send pages to colleagues

Open the SendPages section in OneNote, and then perform the following tasks:

1. Send the sample page to a colleague as an email message attachment.

2. Send the sample page to a colleague as a PDF file.

Share notebooks by using OneDrive

Navigate to the folder that contains the ShareNotebooks section without opening the file, and then perform the following tasks:

1. If necessary, set up a OneDrive account.

2. Sign in to OneDrive and upload the **ShareNotebooks** notebook.

3. Open the **ShareNotebooks** notebook in OneNote Online, and add a note with the text **Additional information to come next week**.

4. Share the **ShareNotebooks** notebook by creating a link that allows your colleagues to edit the file.

5. Share the link to your colleagues in an instant message, email, or shared document.

Share notebooks by using SharePoint

Navigate to the folder that contains the ShareUsingSharePoint section without opening the file, and then perform the following tasks:

1. If necessary, gain access to a SharePoint account.

2. Sign in to SharePoint and upload the **ShareUsingSharePoint** file.

3. Share the **ShareUsingSharePoint** file by sending an email that allows your colleagues to view the file, but not edit it.

Use OneNote with Outlook and Excel

Managing work, school, and home life often means keeping track of meetings and appointments, whether in a physical planner or in Microsoft Outlook. In many cases, you will record task-related information in OneNote, so it's useful that you can create tasks in your OneNote notebook and share them to Outlook. You can also insert meeting information from Outlook into your notebooks, helping you manage your assignments effectively.

OneNote also works well with Microsoft Excel. When you insert an Excel spreadsheet into a notebook page, you can view the spreadsheet, or portions of it, in your notebook and edit the file as required. You can also manage your Microsoft account and your Microsoft Office 365 subscription from OneNote, demonstrating how well OneNote works as part of the Office family.

> ⚠ **IMPORTANT** You must have Outlook and Excel installed to perform some of the procedures and practice tasks in this chapter.

This chapter guides you through procedures related to defining Outlook tasks and displaying meeting details in OneNote; inserting Excel spreadsheets on notebook pages; and managing your Microsoft account, Office 365 subscription, and app settings.

In this chapter

- Define Outlook tasks and display meeting details in OneNote
- Insert Excel spreadsheets on notebook pages
- Manage your Microsoft account, Office 365 subscription, and app settings

Practice files

For this chapter, use the practice files from the OneNoteSBS\Ch09 folder. For practice file download instructions, see the introduction.

Define Outlook tasks and display meeting details in OneNote

OneNote works well in tandem with other Office apps, but it works particularly well with Outlook. For example, if you take notes related to a project and agree to write a summary of a meeting, you can create an Outlook task within your notebook so that it appears in your Reminders list, and you can edit it and save the changes to Outlook. OneNote and Outlook sync some changes, such as the completion status of a task and its start date and due date, but they don't sync changes to the text of the task and note. Finally, if your plans change, you can always delete the task in Outlook or OneNote.

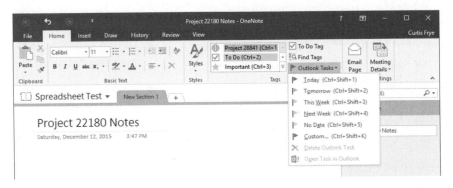

Add Outlook tasks from within OneNote

You can also view information about your upcoming Outlook appointments in OneNote. When you display that information, OneNote shows you today's appointments, but you can move through your appointments one day at a time (including looking back at past events) or select a specific date. If you want to include the details of an appointment on a notebook page, you can do so. As the date of the appointment draws closer, because the dates are synced between the apps, you can update the information inserted into OneNote or Outlook to ensure that it's current.

Insert Outlook appointment information into OneNote

To create an Outlook task from OneNote

1. In OneNote, click the note that you want to create as a task in Outlook.

> **TIP** If you don't click a note, OneNote flags the last note you clicked on the page, or it creates a new note.

2. On the **Home** tab of the ribbon, in the **Tags** group, click **Outlook Tasks**.

3. In the list, click the date you want to perform the task (for example, **Today** or **Tomorrow**). A task is created in Outlook that links back to the note.

4. In the body of the page, if necessary, edit the text of the Outlook task you created.

To open and save an Outlook task in Outlook from OneNote

1. In OneNote, click a note that's tagged as an Outlook task.

2. On the **Home** tab, in the **Tags** group, click **Outlook Tasks**.

3. In the list, click **Open Task in Outlook**.

4. In the Outlook task window, edit the task.

> **TIP** If you mark the task as complete in Outlook or OneNote or if you change the Start Date or Due Date, those changes are synced in both apps. Other changes, such as the text of the task, are not synced.

5. On the **Task** tab of the task window ribbon, in the **Actions** group, click **Save & Close**.

Or

1. In OneNote, right-click an Outlook task flag that's assigned to a note, and click **Open Task in Outlook**.

2. In the Outlook task window, edit the task.

3. On the **Task** tab of the task window ribbon, in the **Actions** group, click **Save & Close**.

To delete an Outlook task from OneNote

1. In OneNote, click a note that's tagged as an Outlook task.

2. On the **Home** tab, in the **Tags** group, click **Outlook Tasks**.

3. In the list, click **Delete Outlook Task**. The task is removed from Outlook and OneNote.

Or

1. In OneNote, right-click an Outlook task flag that's assigned to a note, and click **Delete Outlook Task**.

> **TIP** You can also remove the tag by right-clicking the flag and clicking Remove Tag. The tag is gone, but the task still exists in Outlook.

To view meeting details for the current date from OneNote

1. On the **Home** tab, in the **Meetings** group, click **Meeting Details**. The details about any Outlook meetings you have scheduled for the current date are displayed in the Today's Meetings box.

To view meeting details for another day from OneNote

1. On the **Home** tab, in the **Meetings** group, click **Meeting Details**, and then, at the bottom of the box, click **Choose a Meeting from Another Day**.

2. In the **Insert Outlook Meeting Details** dialog box, do any of the following:

   - Click the **Previous Day** left-pointing arrow to view the previous day's appointments. Repeat as often as necessary to locate the meeting whose details you want to view.

   - Click the **Next Day** right-pointing arrow to view the next day's appointments. Repeat as often as necessary to locate the meeting whose details you want to view.

   - Click the calendar control in the upper-right corner, and use its tools to select the date you want to view.

9

To insert meeting details into OneNote

1. Click on a OneNote notebook page, at the location where you want to insert the meeting details.

2. In the **Insert Outlook Meeting Details** dialog box, use the controls to display the details of the meeting whose information you want to insert.

3. Click the meeting you want to insert.

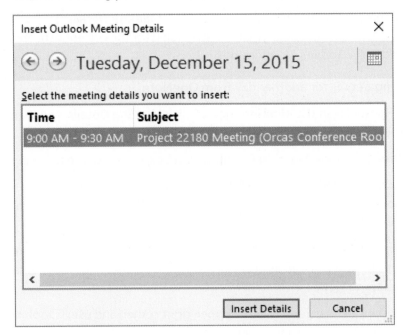

Select a meeting to insert its details into your OneNote notebook

4. Click **Insert Details**.

To refresh details of meetings inserted into OneNote

1. On the **Home** tab, in the **Meetings** group, click **Meeting Details**, and then click **Refresh Meeting Details for This Page** at the bottom of the box.

Insert Excel spreadsheets on notebook pages

OneNote gives you the tools you need to take useful notes to support your projects at work, school, and home. Although you can insert symbols and equations onto your pages, you can't use OneNote on its own to create formulas or advanced calculations.

> **TIP** You can use Excel in OneNote for a lot of great features, but you can also do simple math directly in OneNote. For example, to find the percentage you got on a test on which you received 63 out of 72 points, you can enter "63 / 72 =" and, when you press the spacebar after the equal sign, OneNote will add the answer for you: .0.875, which is 87.5 percent.

Fortunately, Office includes an app that's perfect for the advanced tasks: Excel. Excel is a powerful, flexible tool you can use to organize, summarize, and present your data. If you have Excel installed on your computer, whether as a stand-alone app or as part of an Office 365 subscription, you can insert new or existing Excel spreadsheets onto your notebook pages.

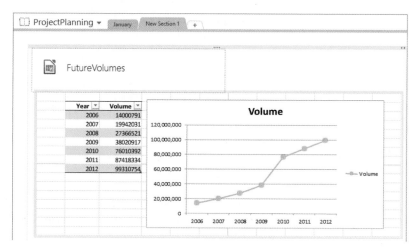

Insert an Excel workbook to analyze numbers in OneNote

Not only can you insert entire Excel files onto your notebook pages, you can elect to insert individual worksheets, or worksheet elements such as charts or Excel tables, into OneNote notebooks. Regardless of which elements you insert, you can edit the file in Excel, rename the inserted spreadsheet, or refresh its contents in OneNote if you suspect the original file has changed. After you insert a spreadsheet, you can also change from showing the entire workbook to selecting specific elements to display.

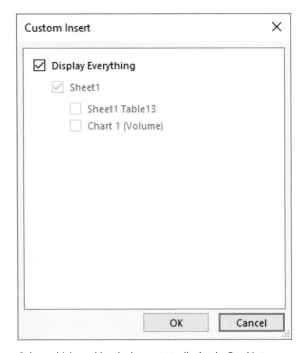

Select which workbook elements to display in OneNote

As with all linked files in OneNote, you can open the original file, copy a link to the file so you can share its address with your colleagues, and delete the file if you no longer need it.

 IMPORTANT Deleting an inserted spreadsheet from a OneNote page does not delete the original file.

To insert a new Excel spreadsheet onto a notebook page

1. Click a location on the notebook page where you want the spreadsheet to be inserted. (If you don't click a location, the spreadsheet will be added as a new note.)

2. On the **Insert** tab of the ribbon, in the **Files** group, click **Spreadsheet**.

3. Click **New Excel Spreadsheet**.

To insert an existing Excel spreadsheet onto a notebook page

1. Click a location on the notebook page where you want the spreadsheet to be inserted.

2. On the **Insert** tab, in the **Files** group, click **Spreadsheet**.

3. Click **Existing Excel Spreadsheet**.

4. In the **Choose Document to Insert** dialog box, navigate to the file you want to insert, select the file, and then click **Insert**.

5. In the **Insert File** dialog box, click **Insert Spreadsheet**.

To insert a single worksheet, a chart, or an Excel table onto a notebook page

1. Click a location on the notebook page where you want the content to be inserted.

2. On the **Insert** tab, in the **Files** group, click **Spreadsheet**.

3. Click **Existing Excel Spreadsheet**.

4. In the **Choose Document to Insert** dialog box, navigate to the file you want to insert, select the file, and then click **Insert**.

5. In the **Insert File** dialog box, click **Insert a Chart or Table**.

6. In the **Custom Insert** dialog box, select the check boxes next to the worksheets or elements you want to insert.

7. Click **OK**.

9

To edit an inserted Excel spreadsheet from within OneNote

1. Point to the inserted spreadsheet, and then click **Edit**.

2. In the Excel app window that appears, edit the spreadsheet. If the spreadsheet is an existing spreadsheet in Excel, this creates a copy of that spreadsheet for you to edit.

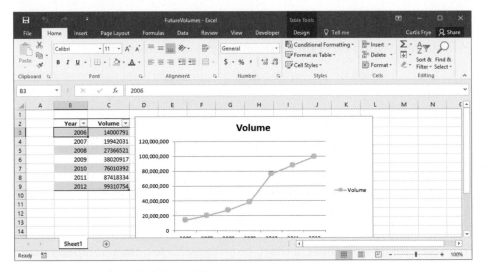

Start editing an Excel workbook from within OneNote

3. In Excel, press **Ctrl+S** to save your work. The OneNote page is updated with your changes.

4. In Excel, click the **Close** button in the upper-right corner of the app window to close Excel and return to OneNote.

To rename an inserted Excel spreadsheet in OneNote

1. Right-click the inserted Excel spreadsheet's icon and file name, and then click **Rename**.

2. In the **Rename File** dialog box, enter a new name for the spreadsheet. The Excel file is saved as a new file.

3. Click **OK**.

To select what to display from an inserted Excel spreadsheet

1. Right-click the inserted Excel spreadsheet, and then click **Select What to Display**.

2. In the **Custom Insert** dialog box, clear the **Display Everything** check box.

3. Select the check boxes next to the elements you want to display.

4. Click **OK**.

To refresh the contents of an inserted Excel spreadsheet

1. Right-click the inserted Excel spreadsheet, and then click **Refresh**.

To open the original version of an inserted Excel spreadsheet

1. Right-click the inserted Excel spreadsheet's icon and file name, and then click **Open Original**.

2. If necessary, in the security warning dialog box that describes the dangers of opening files by using hyperlinks, click **Yes**.

3. In the Excel app window that appears, edit the spreadsheet.

4. In Excel, press **Ctrl+S** to save your work.

5. In Excel, click the **Close** button in the upper-right corner of the app window to close Excel and return to OneNote.

To copy a link to the original version of an inserted Excel spreadsheet

1. Right-click the inserted Excel spreadsheet's icon and file name, and then click **Copy Link to Original**.

2. If the file is online and your colleagues have access, send the link to your colleagues via email or chat, or by inserting the link in a file, such as a Microsoft Word document or PowerPoint presentation.

To delete an inserted Excel spreadsheet

1. Point to the top edge of the note container that includes the inserted spreadsheet.

2. Right-click the title bar of the note container that includes the inserted spreadsheet, and then click **Delete**.

9

Manage your Microsoft account, Office 365 subscription, and app settings

OneNote works well as a stand-alone app, but it works best as part of the Office family of products. You can purchase Office as a set of desktop apps, or you can subscribe to the Office 365 service, which includes the most recent version of Office. To get the most out of OneNote, you should establish a Microsoft account. You can use your Microsoft account to use Microsoft OneDrive, the free online file-sharing service, and other services that require a Microsoft login.

After you establish a Microsoft account, you can add or change the photo associated with the account. A photo helps identify you, by showing either your likeness or a representative image. You can add other information about yourself, such as your phone number or Skype contact details; sign out of your account; or switch to another Microsoft account without signing out. You can also create and manage links to other services, such as Twitter or Facebook, that you connect to your Microsoft account.

In addition to controlling your Microsoft account from within OneNote, you can change settings related to Office as a whole. For example, you can control the appearance of all Office apps by changing the theme and background. These cosmetic settings don't affect how the apps run, but they do change how they look on your screen.

> ⚠ **IMPORTANT** If you purchased Office as a set of stand-alone desktop apps rather than as part of an Office 365 subscription, you will see different information in the Product Information section of the page, but you will still be able to manage your Microsoft account by using the Account page of the Backstage view.

Change your Office 365 Account settings from within OneNote

You also have a great deal of control over how and when Office updates its desktop apps. You can look for updates manually, have Office install updates whenever they are available, or turn off updating entirely. If your Office subscription is a business or other organizational subscription, the organization's information technology department might have set the update policy, so you should check with them if you have any questions.

> ⚠ **IMPORTANT** Office updates include important security and functional changes, so you should keep updates turned on unless your information technology department tells you to turn them off.

9

To change your Microsoft account photo from OneNote

1. In OneNote, click the **File** tab on the ribbon to display the Backstage view, and then click **Account** in the left pane.

2. On the **Account** page, in the **User Information** area, click **Change photo**.

3. If necessary, log on to your Microsoft account.

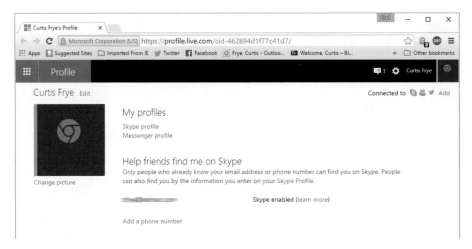

Add contact information to your Microsoft account

4. On the **Profile** page of your account profile, click **Change Picture**.

5. Click **Choose a File**.

6. In the **Open** dialog box, locate the image you want to use, click it, and then click **Open**.

> **IMPORTANT** The image you select must be less than 4 megabytes (MB) in size.

7. Drag the handles on the image preview to select the area of the image to display.

8. Click **Save**.

To change your Microsoft account profile from OneNote

1. In OneNote, on the **Account** page of the Backstage view, in the **User Information** area, click **About Me**.

2. If necessary, log on to your Microsoft account.

3. On the **Profile** page of your account profile, add or edit your phone number, Skype identity, or other information.

4. Click **Save**.

To sign out from your Microsoft account from OneNote

1. In OneNote, on the **Account** page of the Backstage view, click **Sign Out**.

2. In the confirmation dialog box that appears, click **YES**.

To switch to a different Microsoft account from OneNote

1. In OneNote, on the **Account** page of the Backstage view, in the **User Information** area, click **Switch Account**.

2. Click the account to which you want to switch.

Or

1. In OneNote, on the **Account** page of the Backstage view, in the **User Information** area, click **Switch Account**.

2. At the bottom of the **Accounts** dialog box, click **Add Account**.

3. In the **Sign In** dialog box, enter the email address of the account you want to use.

4. If necessary, enter the password of the new account.

5. Press **Enter**.

To add a service from OneNote

1. In the OneNote Backstage view, display the **Account** page. In the **Connected Services** area, at the bottom of the list, click **Add a service**.

2. Click the type of service you want to add.

3. Click the service to add, and follow the prompts to add the service.

9

To manage connected services from OneNote

1. In OneNote, on the **Account** page of the Backstage view, in the **Connected Services** area, click the **Manage** link next to the service you want to manage. A Microsoft account window opens for the service.

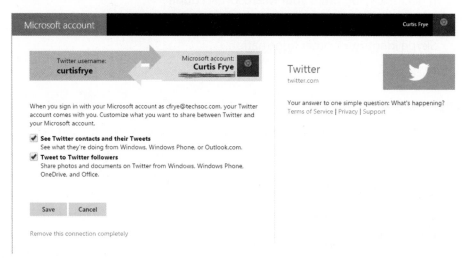

Manage connected services from OneNote

2. In your web browser, do either of the following:

   • Use the available tools to change the service's settings.

   • Click **Remove this connection completely**.

3. Click **Save**.

To change the Office background from OneNote

1. In OneNote, on the **Account** page of the Backstage view, click the **Office Background** list arrow, and then click the background you want to apply. The background design appears in the top title bar of the Office app windows.

Select from a variety of Office backgrounds

9

To change the Office theme from OneNote

1. In OneNote, on the **Account** page of the Backstage view, click the **Office Theme** list arrow, and then click the theme you want to apply. The colors change in the Office apps.

To manage your Office 365 subscription from OneNote

1. In OneNote, on the **Account** page of the Backstage view, under **Subscription Product**, click the **Manage Account** button.

2. If necessary, on the **Office 365 Portal** sign-in page, sign in to your Office 365 account.

3. Use the available tools to manage your account.

To update your Office software from OneNote

1. In OneNote, on the **Account** page of the Backstage view, click **Update Options**.

2. Click **Update Now** to check for available updates.

3. Do either of the following:

   - Follow the prompts in the dialog box that appears, and, if necessary, click **OK** to install any available updates.

   - If the latest updates are all installed on your computer, click **Close**.

To disable updates from OneNote

1. In OneNote, on the **Account** page of the Backstage view, click **Update Options**.

2. Click **Disable Updates**.

3. Click **Yes** to allow Office to make changes to your computer.

To enable updates from OneNote

1. In OneNote, on the **Account** page of the Backstage view, click **Update Options**.

2. If updates are disabled on your computer, click **Enable Updates**.

3. Click **Yes** to allow Office to make changes to your computer.

To view your update history from OneNote

1. In OneNote, on the **Account** page of the Backstage view, click **Update Options**.

2. Click **View Updates**.

3. View the update information page on office.com.

To get more information about updates from OneNote

1. In OneNote, on the **Account** page of the Backstage view, click **Update Options**.

2. Click **About Updates**.

3. Read the information about updates to Office, and then click **OK**.

To get information about OneNote

1. In OneNote, on the **Account** page of the Backstage view, click **About OneNote**.

2. Read the information about OneNote, and then click **OK**.

Skills review

In this chapter, you learned how to:

- Define Outlook tasks and display meeting details in OneNote

- Insert Excel spreadsheets on notebook pages

- Manage your Microsoft account, Office 365 subscription, and app settings

9

Practice tasks

The practice files for these tasks are located in the OneNoteSBS\Ch09 folder. The results of the tasks will be automatically saved into the same file in the same folder.

Define Outlook tasks and display meeting details from OneNote

 IMPORTANT You must have Outlook installed on your computer to complete these tasks.

Open the DefineTasks section in OneNote, start Outlook (if necessary), and then perform the following tasks:

1. In OneNote, create an Outlook task for a meeting to be held tomorrow.

2. Open the task for editing within Outlook, add information such as time and place, and then save and close the task.

3. In OneNote, insert the details of your most recent meeting onto a notebook page.

Insert Excel spreadsheets on notebook pages

 IMPORTANT You must have Excel installed on your computer to complete these tasks.

Open the IncludeSpreadsheets section in OneNote, and then perform the following tasks:

1. Insert the **IdentifyTrends** workbook from the practice file folder into your notebook.

2. Open the **IdentifyTrends** workbook for editing.

3. In worksheet cell **A9**, enter **2015**.

4. In worksheet cell **B9**, enter **92140298**.

5. Save and close the workbook, and then exit Excel.

6. In OneNote, change the inserted spreadsheet's settings so that OneNote displays only the Excel table.

Manage your Microsoft account, Office 365 subscription, and app settings

 IMPORTANT You must have a Microsoft account to complete some of these tasks.

Open the ManageSettings section in OneNote, and then perform the following tasks:

1. Sign in to your Microsoft account and add or change your photo.

2. Change the **Office Background** to a design such as **Circuit** or **Lunchbox**.

3. Change the **Office Theme** to **Dark Gray**.

4. Update your Office installation so it has all available updates applied.

Manage OneNote options and the interface

10

OneNote is designed to be easy to use, with commands laid out on the ribbon so you can discover them easily. Although the way OneNote is installed works perfectly for many users, you might want to change how it responds to your commands. For example, you could show or hide the Mini Toolbar or the Paste Options button, and you can add your name and initials to make tracking changes easier.

You can change the Quick Access Toolbar and the ribbon by adding, moving, and deleting controls. If you find that you use a command such as Print Preview frequently, you can add it to the Quick Access Toolbar so it's readily available. You can also change the ribbon so the tabs and commands you want are displayed where you want them.

This chapter guides you through procedures related to setting OneNote app options, customizing the Quick Access Toolbar, and customizing the ribbon.

In this chapter

- Set OneNote app options
- Customize the Quick Access Toolbar
- Customize the ribbon

Practice files

No practice files are necessary to complete the practice tasks in this chapter.

Set OneNote app options

The Home tab of the ribbon gives you access to a wide variety of formatting tools, but if you're editing text at the bottom of a page, it can take some time to move the pointer to the ribbon and back. To put those formatting and other tools closer to text you've selected, OneNote displays the Mini Toolbar, which contains many formatting tools from the Home tab of the ribbon.

Display the Mini Toolbar to keep formatting tools close at hand

If you prefer that OneNote not display the Mini Toolbar, you can turn it off. You can also determine whether or not OneNote displays information about an app element in a ScreenTip. ScreenTips are small, temporary windows that appear when you point to buttons and other screen elements; they explain what those elements do. If there are keyboard shortcuts available for the feature, the ScreenTip includes that information. Some users prefer to have ScreenTips turned on, whereas others prefer to have them turned off. Regardless of your choice, you can set OneNote to reflect your preference.

If your work requires you to collaborate with others on projects, your organization might use information about who has created and edited Microsoft Office files, so that your colleagues can collaborate with you effectively. Regardless of whether you collaborate with other users by editing shared OneNote notebooks or work by yourself, you should take a moment, if you haven't yet, to enter your name and initials into OneNote. These initials will be used for all the Office apps you work with. Adding this information helps you and your colleagues track who made which changes, facilitating discussion and exploration when you examine a notebook after completing a series of edits.

Other decisions you can make include whether or not to show the OneNote icon on the Windows taskbar, whether to display the page tabs pane (which show the names of pages within a section) on the right or left side of the app window, whether to show or hide note containers (the outlines that appear around notes), and whether the Paste Options button appears on the page after you paste elements from the Clipboard into your notebook.

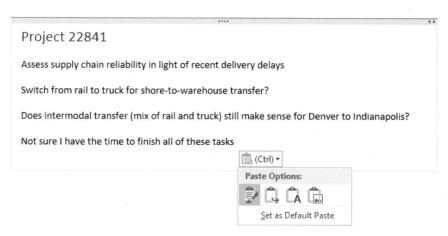

Choose whether OneNote displays the Paste Options button when you paste the contents of the Clipboard into your page

If you create a lot of numbered and bulleted lists in OneNote, you might find it easier to create a numbered list by typing the number 1, followed by a period and a space, to start a list. Similarly, you can start a bulleted list by typing an asterisk or hyphen, followed by a space. These list settings are turned on by default, so if you prefer not to create a numbered or bulleted list when you type either of those text sequences, you can turn off that behavior in OneNote.

To turn the display of the Mini Toolbar off or on

1. Click the **File** tab of the ribbon to display the Backstage view.

2. In the left pane of the Backstage view, click **Options** to open the OneNote Options dialog box.

3. On the **General** page, in the **User Interface Options** area, do either of the following:

   - Clear the **Show Mini Toolbar on selection** check box to turn off the display of the Mini Toolbar when you select text.

   - Select the **Show Mini Toolbar on selection** check box to have OneNote display the Mini Toolbar when you select text.

4. Click **OK**.

To change the display of ScreenTips

1. In the **OneNote Options** dialog box, display the **General** page.

2. In the **User Interface Options** area, click the **ScreenTip style** list arrow, and then do any of the following:

   - Click **Show feature descriptions in ScreenTips** to display ScreenTips that include descriptions of the features.

   - Click **Don't show feature descriptions in ScreenTips** to display ScreenTips that include only the name of the command, without a description.

   - Click **Don't show ScreenTips** to turn off the display of ScreenTips altogether.

3. Click **OK**.

To edit your user name and initials

1. In the **OneNote Options** dialog box, display the **General** page.

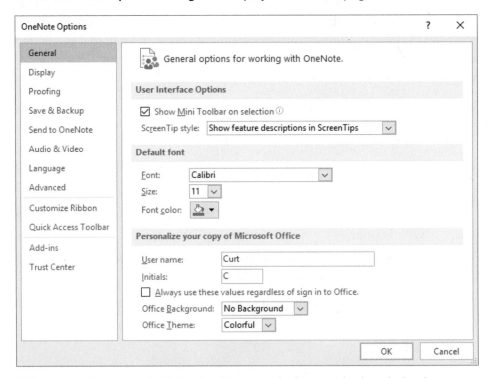

Office apps use the name and initials entered here to track edits to notebooks and other documents

2. In the **User name** box, enter your name.

3. In the **Initials** box, enter the initials you want to use.

 IMPORTANT Editing your user name and initials in OneNote changes those values for every Office app.

4. Click **OK**.

5. A dialog box opens to inform you that you must restart OneNote for the changes to take effect. Click **OK**.

To show or hide the OneNote icon on the Windows taskbar

1. In the **OneNote Options** dialog box, display the **Display** page.

2. Do either of the following to the **Place OneNote icon in the notification area of the taskbar** check box:

   - Select the check box to display the shortcut icon for creating quick notes and displaying screen clippings.

   - Clear the check box to hide the icon.

3. Click **OK**.

To change where the page tabs pane is displayed

1. On the **Display** page of the **OneNote Options** dialog box, do either of the following to the **Page tabs appear on the left** check box:

   - Select the check box to display the page tabs on the left of the app window.

   - Clear the check box to display the page tabs on the right of the app window.

2. Click **OK**.

To show or hide note containers on pages

1. On the **Display** page of the **OneNote Options** dialog box, do either of the following to the **Show note containers on pages** check box:

   - Select the check box to display note containers.

   - Clear the check box to hide note containers.

2. Click **OK**.

 TIP Containers are the borders that appear around each note, or set of paragraphs and objects, on the notebook page. Containers make it easier to format or move notes.

10

To turn the display of the Paste Options button on or off

1. In the **OneNote Options** dialog box, click **Advanced** to display the Advanced page.

2. In the **Editing** area, do either of the following to the **Show Paste Options button when content is pasted** check box:

   - Select the check box to have OneNote display the Paste Options button after you paste text from the Clipboard.

   - Clear the check box to turn off the display of the Paste Options button after you paste text from the Clipboard.

3. Click **OK**.

> **TIP** The paste options give you the choice of keeping the source formatting (the default), merging with the formatting at the destination location, keeping only the text of the content you're pasting, or pasting picture formatting if you're pasting a picture. You can also change the default paste option.

To turn the automatic creation of numbered lists on or off

1. In the **OneNote Options** dialog box, display the **Advanced** page.

2. In the **Editing** area, do either of the following to the **Apply numbering to lists automatically** check box:

   - Select the check box to turn on automatic numbered list creation.

   - Clear the check box to turn off automatic numbered list creation.

3. Click **OK**.

> **TIP** When automatic numbered lists are turned on, you can enter a number, a period, and a space to automatically indent the number and turn the paragraph into a numbered list item.

To turn the automatic creation of bulleted lists on or off

1. In the **OneNote Options** dialog box, display the **Advanced** page.

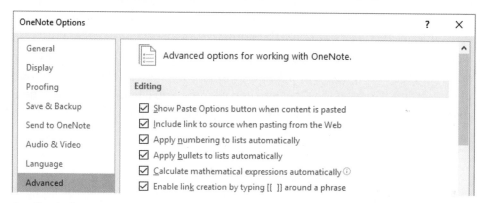

Specify whether OneNote creates bulleted lists automatically

2. In the **Editing** area, do either of the following to the **Apply bullets to lists automatically** check box:

   - Select the check box to turn on automatic bulleted list creation.

   - Clear the check box to turn off automatic bulleted list creation.

3. Click **OK**.

> **TIP** When automatic bulleted lists are turned on, you can enter an asterisk or hyphen, followed by a space, to automatically indent the bullet and turn the paragraph into a bulleted list item.

10

Customize the Quick Access Toolbar

As you continue to work with OneNote, you might discover that you use certain commands much more frequently than others. If your notebooks draw data from external sources, for example, you might find yourself using certain ribbon buttons much more often than other users. You can make any button accessible with one click by adding the button to the Quick Access Toolbar, located just above the ribbon in the upper-left corner of the OneNote app window. You'll find the tools you need to change the buttons on the Quick Access Toolbar in the OneNote Options dialog box.

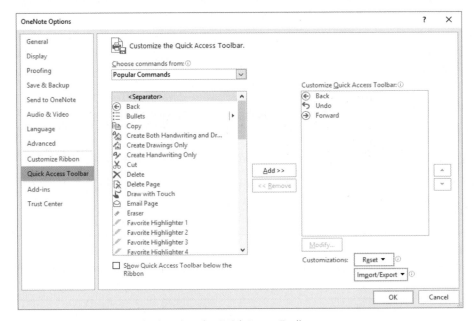

Control which buttons are displayed on the Quick Access Toolbar

You can add buttons to the Quick Access Toolbar, change their positions, and remove them when you no longer need them. Later, if you want to return the Quick Access Toolbar to its original state, you can reset just the Quick Access Toolbar or the entire ribbon interface.

You can also choose whether your Quick Access Toolbar changes affect all your notebooks or just the active notebook. If you'd like to export your Quick Access Toolbar customizations to a file that can be used to apply those changes to another OneNote installation, you can do so quickly.

To add a button to the Quick Access Toolbar

1. In the **OneNote Options** dialog box, click **Quick Access Toolbar** to display the Quick Access Toolbar page.

2. In the **Choose commands from** list, click the category of commands from which you want to choose.

3. In the **Choose commands from** pane, do either of the following to add a command to the Customize Quick Access Toolbar pane:

   - Click the command you want to add to the Quick Access Toolbar, and then click the **Add** button between the two lists.

   - Double-click the command you want to add to the Quick Access Toolbar.

4. Click **OK**.

To change the order of buttons on the Quick Access Toolbar

1. In the **OneNote Options** dialog box, display the **Quick Access Toolbar** page.

2. In the **Customize Quick Access Toolbar** pane, click the button you want to move.

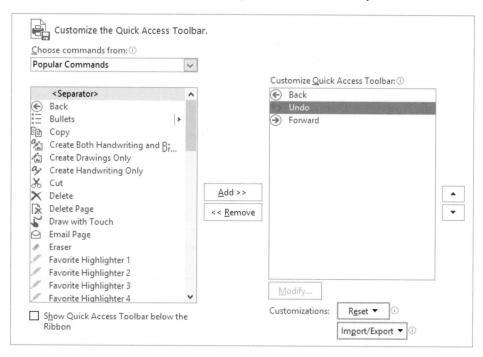

10

Change the order of buttons on the Quick Access Toolbar

3. To the right of the **Customize Quick Access Toolbar** pane, do either of the following:

   - Click the **Move Up** button to move the button higher in the list and to the left on the Quick Access Toolbar.

   - Click the **Move Down** button to move the button lower in the list and to the right on the Quick Access Toolbar.

4. Repeat steps 2 and 3 until the buttons are in the order you want.

5. Click **OK**.

To remove a button from the Quick Access Toolbar

1. In the **OneNote Options** dialog box, display the **Quick Access Toolbar** page.

2. In the **Customize Quick Access Toolbar** pane, do either of the following:

   - Click the command you want to remove from the Quick Access Toolbar, and then click the **Remove** button between the two panes.

   - Double-click the button you want to remove from the Quick Access Toolbar.

3. Click **OK**.

To export your Quick Access Toolbar settings to a file

1. In the **OneNote Options** dialog box, display the **Quick Access Toolbar** page.

2. Click **Import/Export**, and then click **Export all customizations**.

3. In the **File Save** dialog box, navigate to the folder where you want to place the customizations file.

4. In the **File name** box, enter a name for the settings file.

5. Click **Save**.

 TIP This operation exports all your customizations for both the ribbon and Quick Access Toolbar.

To import the Quick Access Toolbar settings from a file

1. In the **OneNote Options** dialog box, display the **Quick Access Toolbar** page.

2. Click **Import/Export**, and then click **Import customization file**.

3. In the **File Open** dialog box, navigate to the folder that contains the customization file, and then click the file.

4. Click **Open**.

5. In the **OneNote Options** dialog box, click **OK**.

To reset the Quick Access Toolbar to its original configuration

1. In the **OneNote Options** dialog box, display the **Quick Access Toolbar** page.

2. Below the **Customize Quick Access Toolbar** pane, click the **Reset** button.

3. Do either of the following:

   - Click **Reset only Quick Access Toolbar**.

   - Click **Reset all customizations** to reset both the Quick Access Toolbar configuration and the ribbon configuration.

4. Click **OK**.

10

Customize the ribbon

You can easily customize the entire ribbon in OneNote by hiding and displaying ribbon tabs, reordering tabs that are displayed on the ribbon, customizing existing tabs (including tool tabs, which appear when specific items are selected), and creating custom tabs. You'll find the tools to customize the ribbon in the OneNote Options dialog box.

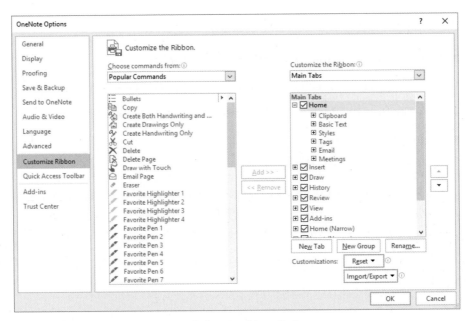

Control the tabs, groups, and commands that the ribbon displays

From the Customize Ribbon page of the OneNote Options dialog box, you can select which tabs are displayed on the ribbon and in what order. In the right pane, each ribbon tab name has a check box next to it. If a check box is selected, that tab appears on the ribbon.

Just as you can change the order of the tabs on the ribbon, you can change the order of the groups of commands on a tab.

For example, the History tab contains three groups: Unread, Authors, and History. If you use the History group more frequently than the other groups, you could move it to the left end of the tab.

Change the order of items on built-in ribbon tabs

You can also remove groups from a ribbon tab. If you remove a group from a built-in tab and later decide you want to restore it, you can put it back without too much trouble.

The built-in ribbon tabs are designed for maximum efficiency, so adding new command groups might crowd the other items on the tab and make those controls harder to find. Rather than adding controls to an existing ribbon tab, you can create a custom tab and then add groups and commands to it. The default New Tab (Custom) name doesn't tell you anything about the commands on your new ribbon tab, so you can rename it to reflect its contents.

 TIP You can change the order of the groups and commands on your custom ribbon tabs by using the same techniques that are used for the built-in tabs.

You can export your ribbon customizations to a file that can be used to apply those changes to another OneNote installation. When you're ready to apply saved customizations to OneNote, you can then import the file and apply them. And, as with the Quick Access Toolbar, you can always reset the ribbon to its original state.

The ribbon is designed to use space efficiently, but you can hide it if you want to increase the amount of space available inside the app window.

10

To display a ribbon tab

1. In the **OneNote Options** dialog box, click **Customize Ribbon** to display the Customize Ribbon page.

2. In the **Customize the Ribbon** pane on the right side of the page, select the check box next to the name of the tab you want to display.

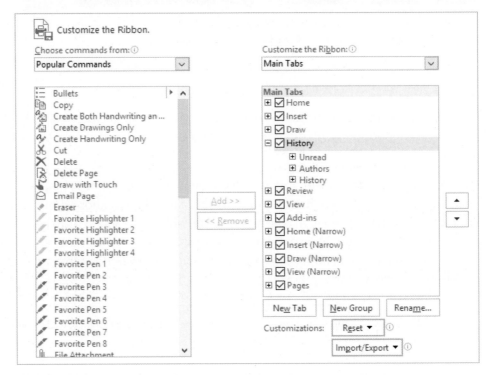

Select the check box next to the tab you want to display on the ribbon

3. Click **OK**.

To hide a ribbon tab

1. In the **OneNote Options** dialog box, display the **Customize Ribbon** page.

2. In the **Customize the Ribbon** pane on the right side of the page, clear the check box next to the name of the tab you want to hide.

3. Click **OK**.

To reorder ribbon tabs and groups

> **TIP** You can't move individual commands on the built-in tabs; you can move only groups and tabs.

1. In the **OneNote Options** dialog box, display the **Customize Ribbon** page.

2. If you want to reorder the groups on a tab, first display the groups by clicking the expand list button (the plus sign) to the left of the tab.

3. In the ribbon elements list, click the element (tab or group) you want to move.

4. To the right of the list, do either of the following:

    *   Click the **Move Up** button to move the element higher in the list and to the left on the ribbon tab.

    *   Click the **Move Down** button to move the element lower in the list and to the right on the ribbon tab.

5. Repeat steps 3 and 4 until the elements are in the order you want.

6. Click **OK**.

To create a custom ribbon tab

1. In the **OneNote Options** dialog box, display the **Customize Ribbon** page.

2. Below the list on the right, click the **New Tab** button. The new tab, named *New Tab (Custom)*, is added to the list on the right. It contains one group, named *New Group (Custom)*.

To create a custom group on a ribbon tab

1. In the **OneNote Options** dialog box, display the **Customize Ribbon** page.

2. If necessary, in the list on the right, click the expand list button (the plus sign) to the left of the tab on which you want to add the custom group, to display the groups on the tab.

3. In the list on the right, click the ribbon tab on which you want to create the custom group.

4. Click **New Group**. The new group, named *New Group (Custom)*, is added to the tab in the location you indicated.

10

To add a button to a custom group on the ribbon

1. In the **OneNote Options** dialog box, display the **Customize Ribbon** page.

2. In the **Customize the Ribbon** list, click **Main Tabs**, **Tool Tabs**, or **All Tabs** to display those tabs in the adjacent pane.

3. In the **Customize the Ribbon** pane, click the custom group to which you want to add a button.

4. In the **Choose commands from** list, click a category to display those commands in the adjacent pane.

5. In the **Choose commands from** pane, click the command you want to add to the ribbon.

6. Click the **Add** button between the two panes to add the button to the Customize The Ribbon pane and to the ribbon.

7. Click **OK**.

To rename a ribbon element

1. In the **OneNote Options** dialog box, display the **Customize Ribbon** page.

2. In the **Customize the Ribbon** pane, click the ribbon tab, group, or command you want to rename.

3. Below the **Customize the Ribbon** pane, click the **Rename** button.

4. In the **Rename** dialog box, do the following:

   a. In the **Display name** box, enter a new name for the ribbon element.

   b. If you are renaming a group or command and want to change its symbol, select a symbol from the **Symbol** gallery.

   c. Click **OK**.

5. In the **OneNote Options** dialog box, click **OK**.

To remove an element from the ribbon

1. In the **OneNote Options** dialog box, display the **Customize Ribbon** page.

2. In the **Customize the Ribbon** pane, click the ribbon tab, group, or command you want to remove.

3. Click the **Remove** button between the two panes to remove the button from the Customize The Ribbon pane and from the ribbon.

4. Click **OK**.

To export your ribbon customizations to a file

1. In the **OneNote Options** dialog box, display the **Customize Ribbon** page.

2. Click **Import/Export**, and then click **Export all customizations**.

3. In the **File Save** dialog box, navigate to the folder in which you want to save the customizations file, and then in the **File name** box, enter a name for the settings file.

4. Click **Save**.

To import ribbon customizations from a file

1. In the **OneNote Options** dialog box, display the **Customize Ribbon** page.

2. Click **Import/Export**, and then click **Import customization file**.

3. In the **File Open** dialog box, navigate to and click the configuration file, and then click **Open**.

4. In the **OneNote Options** dialog box, click **OK**.

To reset the ribbon to its original configuration

1. In the **OneNote Options** dialog box, display the **Customize Ribbon** page.

2. If you want to reset only one tab, select the tab in the list on the right.

3. Below the list, click the **Reset** button.

10

4. Do either of the following:

    -   Click **Reset only selected Ribbon tab** to reset the selected tab's customizations and to remove all the groups and commands you added to that tab.

    -   Click **Reset all customizations** to reset all the ribbon tabs and Quick Access Toolbar customizations and to remove all custom tabs, groups, and commands.

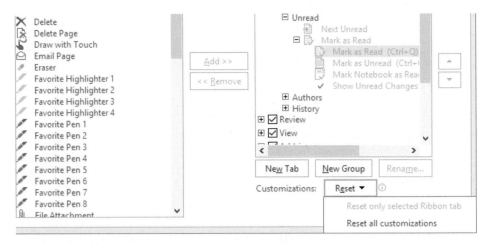

Reset the ribbon and Quick Access Toolbar to their original settings

5. In the dialog box that opens, click **Yes**.

To hide or unhide the ribbon

1. To hide the ribbon, in the lower-right corner of the ribbon, click the **Collapse the Ribbon** arrow.

2. To unhide the ribbon, click a tab to temporarily open the ribbon, and then click the **Pin the ribbon** pushpin in the lower-right corner of the ribbon.

Or

1. Press **Ctrl+F1**.

Skills review

In this chapter, you learned how to:

- Set OneNote app options
- Customize the Quick Access Toolbar
- Customize the ribbon

10

Practice tasks

No practice files are necessary to complete the practice tasks in this chapter.

Set OneNote app options

Open any notebook in OneNote, and then perform the following tasks:

1. Display the **General** page of the **OneNote Options** dialog box.

2. Enter values for your user name and initials.

3. On the **Advanced** page of the **OneNote Options** dialog box, clear the **Show Paste Options button when content is pasted** check box.

4. Clear the **Apply bullets to lists automatically** check box.

5. Click **OK** to save your changes, or click **Cancel** to leave the OneNote options as they were before you opened the dialog box.

> **TIP** If you plan to continue working in OneNote, you should click Cancel so the app's behavior is unchanged.

Customize the Quick Access Toolbar

Open any notebook in OneNote, and then perform the following tasks:

1. Display the **Quick Access Toolbar** page of the **OneNote Options** dialog box.

2. From the **Popular Commands** category, add the **Bullets** and **Print Preview** buttons to the Quick Access Toolbar.

3. Move the **Print Preview** button to the left end of the Quick Access Toolbar.

4. Remove the **Bullets** button from the Quick Access Toolbar.

5. Reset only the Quick Access Toolbar to its original configuration.

Customize the ribbon

Open any notebook in OneNote, and then perform the following tasks:

1. Display the **Customize Ribbon** page of the **OneNote Options** dialog box.

2. Move the **Review** tab to the left end of the ribbon.

3. On the **View** tab of the ribbon, move the **Window** group to the leftmost position on the tab.

Enhance OneNote by using the Onetastic add-in

OneNote is a useful and flexible app, but developers have found ways to enhance its capabilities. The Onetastic add-in, which was developed by a member of the Microsoft OneNote team, adds macros to the OneNote ribbon, giving you tools that you can use to perform tasks.

For example, you can view and manage your notebook pages by using a calendar utility called OneCalendar, or crop an image within OneNote. You can also take advantage of extended and powerful page management capabilities, such as adding frequently visited pages to a favorites list, and defining custom styles that you can use to quickly format your page text. The Onetastic add-in also provides additional ways to search and manage page text, images, and tables; and to quickly remove hyperlinks and author history information before sharing notebook pages.

> **IMPORTANT** The Onetastic add-in is not a part of OneNote and is not a Microsoft product.

This chapter guides you through procedures related to downloading and installing the Onetastic add-in; managing notebooks by using OneCalendar; managing pages and styles by using Onetastic; and managing content, images, and tables by using Onetastic.

In this chapter

- Download and install the Onetastic add-in
- Manage notebooks by using OneCalendar
- Manage pages and styles by using Onetastic
- Manage content, images, and tables by using Onetastic

Practice files

For this chapter, use the practice files from the OneNoteSBS\Ch11 folder. For practice file download instructions, see the introduction.

Download and install the Onetastic add-in

The Onetastic add-in, which adds a set of useful functions to OneNote, was developed by Omer Atay, a software developer on the OneNote team. You can download the add-in and find helpful resources such as Onetastic documentation, Atay's blog, and collections of tools that enhance the capabilities of OneNote from the Onetastic for Microsoft OneNote site at *www.omeratay.com/onetastic*.

Visit the main Onetastic site to download the add-in

Onetastic comes in two varieties, 32-bit and 64-bit, which correspond to the specific version of Microsoft Office that you're running. Unless you work in a scientific or high-end business analysis field, you most likely have the 32-bit version of Office installed on your computer. You can quickly verify which version of Office you're running so you can be sure to download the correct file.

 IMPORTANT Even if you have a 64-bit version of Windows installed on your computer, you are still likely to be running the 32-bit version of Office.

After you download and unzip the Onetastic installer, you can add Onetastic to OneNote and start using its additional capabilities.

> ⚠ **IMPORTANT** You can find helpful information about Onetastic installation and answers to common questions on the Frequently Asked Questions page available through *www.omeratay.com/onetastic*.

To check whether you are running 32-bit or 64-bit Office

1. In OneNote, click the **File** tab of the ribbon to display the Backstage view.

2. In the left pane of the Backstage view, click **Account** to display the Account page.

3. In the **Subscription Product** area on the right side of the page, click the **About OneNote** button.

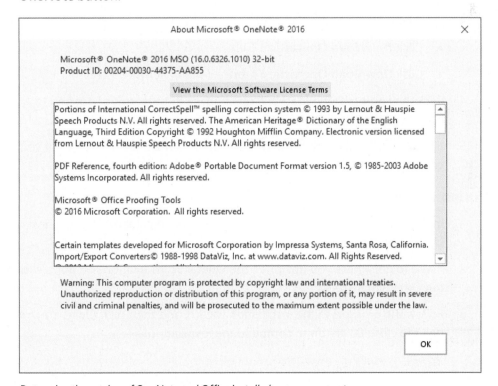

Determine the version of OneNote and Office installed on your computer

4. In the **About Microsoft OneNote 2016** dialog box, look for *32-bit* or *64-bit* at the end of the app description in the first line of text within the dialog box. You'll use this information to determine whether you download the 32-bit or 64-bit version of Onetastic.

 IMPORTANT You can't mix 32-bit and 64-bit Office apps on your computer, so your version of OneNote must match that of Office.

5. Click **OK**.

To download Onetastic

1. In your web browser, go to *www.omeratay.com/onetastic/*.

2. Click **Download Now**.

3. On the **Download** page, do either of the following:

   - Click **Download Onetastic 32-bit**.

   - Click **Download Onetastic 64-bit**.

4. Click the **I agree, Download** button to agree to the terms of use and to download the installation file.

5. In your web browser, save the **OnetasticInstaller** zip file to a folder of your choice.

To install Onetastic

1. In File Explorer, display the folder to which you downloaded the Onetastic installation file, and unzip it.

2. In the folder where you unzipped the Onetastic installation file, double-click the **OnetasticInstaller** file.

3. Follow the prompts in the installation wizard, and then click **Close**. You might need to close OneNote to complete the installation.

Manage notebooks by using OneCalendar

As your OneNote notebooks grow, so will the number of pages they contain. You can use OneCalendar, an add-in that is part of the Onetastic installation, to display your pages by creation date and last-modified date. You can organize your pages by month, week, or day.

 TIP OneCalendar is also available as a separate download from the Onetastic website.

View all pages created or last modified on specific days in a month

If you use OneNote to track multiple projects and create a lot of pages at one time, the monthly view for OneCalendar might not provide enough room to display all of the pages in a day's box at once. If that's the case, you can display the additional pages quickly. You can also navigate through the calendar, moving to months, weeks, or days in sequence, or selecting a specific month and year to show in OneCalendar. If you want to see pages created or last modified on the current day, you can display them with a single click. If you want to limit OneCalendar's summary to just those pages that contain a specific word or phrase, you can filter the display to focus on what's important to you.

11

As with OneNote itself, you can change the OneCalendar add-in's settings to customize it for your use. For example, you can change the font size used to display page results, start the week on Monday instead of Sunday, or select the add-in's language from a list of more than a dozen possibilities.

Select the language to use in OneCalendar

Other settings include the ability to turn on or off the page previews that appear when you point to a page's hyperlink, display pages based on the date created or last modified (or both), and select which notebooks to include in the OneCalendar display.

To launch OneCalendar for the first time

1. In OneNote, on the **Home** tab of the ribbon, in the **Tools** group, click the **Launch OneCalendar** button.

2. In the OneCalendar window, on the **Language** page, click the language you want to use.

3. Click **Continue** to complete the OneCalendar setup.

> **TIP** OneCalendar starts each time you start OneNote, which might take some time. You might want to leave OneNote open if you're going to use it repeatedly.

To navigate to a page in OneCalendar

1. On the **Home** tab, click the **Launch OneCalendar** button to start OneCalendar.

2. Click the hyperlink representing the page you want to view.

To change the time period displayed in OneCalendar

1. To display a month, do either of the following:

    - In the lower-right corner of the OneCalendar window, click the **Month** button.

    - Press **Ctrl+1**.

2. To display a week, do either of the following:

    - In the lower-right corner of the OneCalendar window, click the **Week** button.

    - Press **Ctrl+2**.

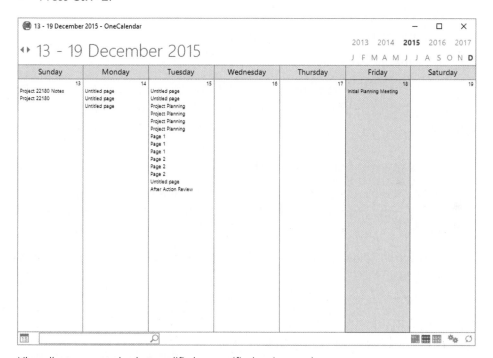

View all pages created or last modified on specific days in a week

3. To display a day, do either of the following:

    - In the lower-right corner of the OneCalendar window, click the **Day** button.

    - Press **Ctrl+3**.

 TIP Displaying page dates by month is the default state for OneCalendar.

To navigate through time periods in OneCalendar

1. To display the previous month, week, or day, do either of the following:

    *   In the upper-left corner of the OneCalendar window, click the **Previous** button.

    *   Press **Ctrl+Left Arrow**.

2. To display the next month, week, or day, do either of the following:

    *   In the upper-left corner of the OneCalendar window, click the **Next** button.

    *   Press **Ctrl+Right Arrow**.

To display the current date in OneCalendar

1. Display the Day view of OneCalendar.

2. Do either of the following:

    *   In the lower-left corner of the OneCalendar window, click the **Go to Today** button.

    *   Press **Ctrl+0**.

To display a specific month in OneCalendar

1. If the month is in a year other than the one that is currently displayed, in the upper-right corner of the OneCalendar window, click the year you want to display.

2. In the area below the years, click the letter that represents the month you want to display.

Select the month and year to display in OneCalendar

To display hidden pages

1. In any OneCalendar view, point to the day that contains undisplayed pages.

2. Click the arrow that appears.

To filter the pages shown in OneCalendar

1. In the lower-left corner of the OneCalendar window, enter the filter value (for example, *shipping*) in the **Instant Search** box, and then press **Enter**.

To remove a OneCalendar filter

1. In the lower-left corner of the OneCalendar window, delete the contents of the **Instant Search** box.

To display pages by date created or last modified

1. In OneCalendar, do either of the following to display the Settings page:

   - In the lower-right corner of the OneCalendar window, click the **Settings** button.

   - Press **Ctrl+S**.

2. On the **Settings** page of OneCalendar, in the **Show Pages On** area, do either of the following:

   - Select the **Created Date** check box to display pages in OneCalendar views on the date they were created.

   - Select the **Last Modified Date** check box to display pages in OneCalendar views on the date they were last modified.

    TIP You can select both check boxes to show pages both on their created dates and on their last-modified dates.

3. Do either of the following to return to the calendar:

   - Click the **Back** arrow to the left of the **Settings** title.

   - Press **Esc**.

11

To start the weekly OneCalendar display on Monday

1. In OneCalendar, do either of the following to display the Settings page:

   - In the lower-right corner of the OneCalendar window, click the **Settings** button.

   - Press **Ctrl+S**.

Change font size, page display, and other settings in OneCalendar

2. On the **Settings** page of OneCalendar, in the **Other** area, select the **Week starts with Monday** check box.

3. Do either of the following to return to the calendar:

   - Click the **Back** arrow to the left of the **Settings** title.

   - Press **Esc**.

To turn page previews on or off

> **TIP** By default, OneCalendar displays a page preview when you point to a page link on a calendar date. You can use the steps in this procedure to turn that behavior off or back on if it has been turned off.

1. In OneCalendar, do either of the following to display the Settings page:

   - In the lower-right corner of the OneCalendar window, click the **Settings** icon.

   - Press **Ctrl+S**.

2. On the **Settings** page, in the **Other** area, do either of the following:

   - Select the **Show page previews on hover** check box to turn on page previews.

   - Clear the **Show page previews on hover** check box to turn off page previews.

3. Do either of the following to return to the calendar:

   - Click the **Back** arrow to the left of the **Settings** title.

   - Press **Esc**.

11

To change the language used in OneCalendar

1. In OneCalendar, do either of the following to display the Settings page:

    *   In the lower-right corner of the OneCalendar window, click the **Settings** button.

    *   Press **Ctrl+S**.

2. On the **Settings** page of OneCalendar, in the **Language** area, click the language you want to use.

3. Do either of the following to return to the calendar:

    *   Click the **Back** arrow to the left of the **Settings** title.

    *   Press **Esc**.

To change the OneCalendar font size

1. In OneCalendar, do either of the following to display the Settings page:

    *   In the lower-right corner of the OneCalendar window, click the **Settings** icon, which looks like a pair of gears.

    *   Press **Ctrl+S**.

2. On the **Settings** page of OneCalendar, in the **Font Size** area, click the size you want to apply.

3. Do either of the following to return to the calendar:

    *   Click the **Back** arrow to the left of the **Settings** title.

    *   Press **Esc**.

To select which notebooks to include in the OneCalendar summary

1. In OneCalendar, do either of the following to display the Settings page:

   - In the lower-right corner of the OneCalendar window, click the **Settings** button.

   - Press **Ctrl+S**.

2. On the **Settings** page of OneCalendar, in the **Notebooks** area, do either of the following:

   - Click **All Notebooks**.

   - Click **Selected Notebooks**, and then select the check boxes next to the notebooks you want to include in the calendar summary. If necessary, scroll down to display more notebooks.

3. Do either of the following to return to the calendar:

   - Click the **Back** arrow to the left of the **Settings** title.

   - Press **Esc**.

To refresh the pages in the OneCalendar summary

1. In OneNote, on the **Home** tab, click **Launch OneCalendar**.

2. Do either of the following:

   - In the lower-right corner of the OneCalendar window, click the **Refresh** icon.

   - Press **F5**.

> **TIP** If you make changes to OneNote notes while OneCalendar is open, you can refresh OneCalendar to get the current change information. After you start the refresh process, OneCalendar will load all the information again, so it could take a while.

To close OneCalendar

1. In the upper-right corner of the OneCalendar window, click the **Close** button.

11

Manage pages and styles by using Onetastic

The page and section navigation tools that are part of OneNote provide a useful and intuitive way to move among pages, but Onetastic offers additional resources. For example, you can pin pages or sections to the desktop, which helps you find them quickly, regardless of which apps you have open, or you can pin pages or sections to the Onetastic favorites list.

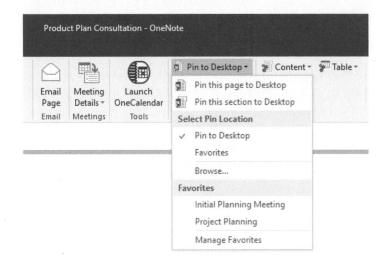

Add favorites to the OneNote ribbon

> **IMPORTANT** Under Select Pin Location, in the list that is displayed when you click the button, you can select whether to pin a page or section to the desktop or to the favorites list. The Pin To Desktop and Pin to Favorites functionalities are two states of the same button; the one that is active depends on whether you have selected Pin To Desktop or Favorites in the list. You can switch the button states without affecting the display of the changes.

Onetastic also enhances your ability to work with text styles. OneNote includes a wide variety of styles you can use for headings and content, but you aren't able to create custom styles based on existing text. Onetastic provides that capability. By using Onetastic, you can define new custom styles based on existing text, apply those styles to your page content, and delete styles you no longer need.

To pin a page to the desktop

1. On the **Home** tab, in the **Onetastic** group, click the **Pin to Desktop** button, and then click **Pin this page to Desktop**. A shortcut to the page appears on the Windows desktop.

 TIP If the button is set to Pin To Favorites, click it, and then in the list, under Select Pin Location, click Pin To Desktop to change the button's name to Pin To Desktop. Then follow the instructions in step 1.

To pin a section to the desktop

1. On the **Home** tab, in the **Onetastic** group, click the **Pin to Desktop** button, and then click **Pin this section to Desktop**. The section appears as a shortcut on the Windows desktop.

To pin a page or section to the Onetastic Favorites list

1. If necessary, on the **Home** tab, in the **Onetastic** group, click the **Pin to Desktop** button, and then click **Favorites**.

 TIP If the button is already set to Pin To Favorites, you can skip this first step.

2. On the **Home** tab, in the **Onetastic** group, click the **Pin to Favorites** button, and then do either of the following:

   • To pin a page to the list, click **Pin this page to Favorites**.

   • To pin a section to the list, click **Pin this section to Favorites**.

   The page or section appears as an item in the Favorites section at the bottom of the Pin To Favorites list that you just opened.

To display a page or section from the Onetastic Favorites list

1. On the **Home** tab, in the **Onetastic** group, click the **Pin to Desktop** or **Pin to Favorites** button. (The name of the button depends on its setting; both variations display the Favorites section.)

2. In the list, in the **Favorites** section, click the page or section you want to display.

11

To manage Onetastic favorites

1. On the **Home** tab, in the **Onetastic** group, click the **Pin to Desktop** or **Pin to Favorites** button.

2. In the list, in the **Favorites** section, click **Manage Favorites**.

3. In the File Explorer dialog box that opens, rename or delete the favorites displayed in the dialog box. The changes are automatically synced in the Pin To Desktop/Favorites list.

> **TIP** Using this technique to rename or delete a section or page that is pinned to Favorites does not rename or delete the section or page in OneNote.

4. Click the **Close** button in the upper-right corner of File Explorer to close it.

To create a custom style

1. On a notebook page, format text to reflect the appearance you want to save as a custom style, and then click or select part of the formatted text.

2. On the **Home** tab, in the **Onetastic** group, click **Custom Styles**, and then click **Save Selection as Custom Style**.

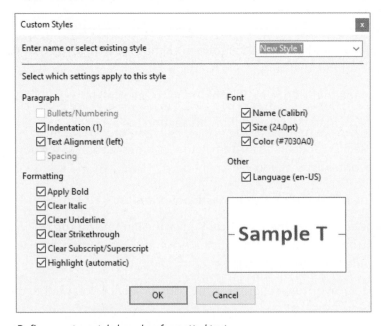

Define a custom style based on formatted text

3. In the **Custom Styles** dialog box, in the **Enter name or select existing style** box, enter a name for the style.

4. In the **Select which settings apply to this style** section of the dialog box, select the check boxes next to the aspects of the style you want to record.

5. Click **OK**.

To apply a custom style

1. On a notebook page, select the text to which you want to apply a custom style.

2. On the **Home** tab, in the **Onetastic** group, click **Custom Styles**, and then click the style you want to apply.

To delete a custom style

1. On the **Home** tab, in the **Onetastic** group, click **Custom Styles**, and then click **Manage Custom Styles**.

> **TIP** You can't edit a Onetastic custom style. Instead, apply the style you want to change to your text, make the style changes directly to that text, and then save the changes as a new custom style (see the procedure "To create a custom style" earlier in this topic).

2. In the **Custom Styles** dialog box, click the **Select an existing style** list arrow, and then, from the alphabetical list of styles, click the style you want to delete.

3. Click **Delete**.

4. In the **Delete Custom Style** dialog box, click **Yes**.

5. In the upper-right corner of the **Custom Styles** dialog box, click **Close**.

11

Manage content, images, and tables by using Onetastic

OneNote maintains a record of which author entered which notes. You can use this functionality to identify the source of specific changes and, if necessary, search for notes created by a colleague.

 SEE ALSO For more information about viewing notes by author, see "Review notes by author and read status" in Chapter 6, "Manage views, windows, and page versions."

For some projects, it might be better to remove author information and other metadata, such as hyperlinks, so the notebook can be shared without revealing too much about the process that went into creating it. Removing author indicators and hyperlinks can be done within OneNote, but you can use Onetastic to perform either of those tasks by making a single selection from the ribbon.

You can also work with your pages' contents by increasing or decreasing the font size of all text, not just the text that is currently selected. You can also highlight or replace text of your choosing.

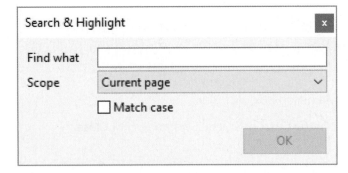

Search for and highlight text in your notebooks

Just as you can resize your notebooks' text, you can use the additional capabilities of Onetastic to select and resize images by specifying a percentage of their current size, a procedure that is not available within OneNote. If you work with tables, which are terrific for maintaining sets of data, you can create simple formulas to find the sum, average, or other summary of the values in your page.

To remove author information from the current page

1. On the **Home** tab, in the **Macros** group, click **Content**, and then click **Clean Authors**. All the edits and notes on that page no longer include author history information.

> **TIP** To quickly test the results, right-click any object on that page. At the bottom of the shortcut menu, the name of the person who made the last edit to that object will no longer be displayed—only the time is displayed. You can test this on other pages to see the differences.

To remove hyperlinks from the current page

1. On the **Home** tab, in the **Macros** group, click **Content**, and then click **Clean Hyperlinks**. All the hyperlinks are removed from the page, but the text and objects are not changed.

> **TIP** You can't remove hyperlinks if the URL is written out in the note. This feature removes only embedded links. For example, the text *www.onenote.com* will display as a link, and the link won't be removed by this feature. Instead, you can remove those links manually or embed links within text instead of writing out the URL as the text.

To increase the font size on the current page

1. Do either of the following:

   - On the **Home** tab, in the **Macros** group, click **Content**, and then click **Increase Font Size**.

   - Press **Ctrl+Plus sign** (on the numeric keypad).

> **IMPORTANT** If you use this feature to increase or decrease the font size on a page, you'll remove all the math equations from the page.

To decrease the font size on the current page

1. Do either of the following:

   - On the **Home** tab, in the **Macros** group, click **Content**, and then click **Decrease Font Size**.

   - Press **Ctrl+Minus sign** (on the numeric keypad).

11

To search for and highlight text on the current page

1. Display the page on which you want to search for and highlight text.

2. On the **Home** tab, in the **Macros** group, click **Find**, and then click **Search & Highlight**.

3. In the **Search & Highlight** dialog box, in the **Find what** box, enter the text for which you want to search.

4. Click the **Scope** list arrow, and then click **Current page** to search on your current page, or click **Selection** if you've selected text you want to find within the current page.

> **IMPORTANT** If no content is selected, you can still search by using the Selection scope, but you'll get no results.

5. If necessary, select the **Match case** check box.

6. Click **OK**.

7. In the confirmation dialog box that opens, click **OK**.

> **TIP** This search function doesn't search the text in images.

To search for and replace text

1. Display the page on which you want to search for and replace text.

2. On the **Home** tab, in the **Macros** group, click **Find**, and then click **Search & Replace**.

3. In the **Search & Replace** dialog box, in the **Find what** box, enter the text for which you want to search.

4. In the **Replace with** box, enter the text you want to substitute for the found text.

5. In the **Scope** list, click the scope for the search (**Current page**, **Selection**, **Current section**, **Current notebooks**, or **All notebooks**).

6. If necessary, select the **Match case** check box.

7. Click **OK**.

8. In the confirmation dialog box that opens, click **OK**.

To select all images on a page

1. On the **Home** tab, in the **Macros** group, click **Image**, and then click **Select Images**.

 IMPORTANT If you select all of the images on a page, you'll remove all the math equations from the page.

To resize all images on a page

1. On the **Home** tab in the **Macros** group, click **Image**, and then click **Resize Images**.

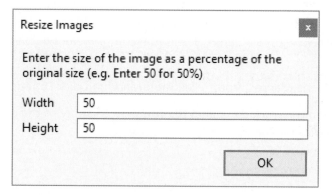

Change the size of all the images on a page in OneNote

2. In the **Resize Images** dialog box, in the **Width** box, enter a new width for the image expressed as a percentage of its current width.

3. In the **Height** box, type a new height for the image expressed as a percentage of its current height.

 IMPORTANT Enter the new width and height as numbers, omitting the percent symbol (for example, enter 75 percent as 75, not 75%). If you enter different numbers in the width and height boxes, the aspect ratio changes.

4. Click **OK**.

 IMPORTANT The changes apply to all the images on the page. To resize an individual image, select the image, and then drag one of the size handles (the squares on the corners).

11

To crop an image

1. On any page in OneNote, right-click an image, and then click **Crop**.

2. Move the purple image border handles to display the part of the image that you want to keep.

3. Click **Accept**.

To add a function to a table

 IMPORTANT This procedure applies to OneNote tables, not Excel worksheets included in a OneNote page.

1. Select the OneNote table cell or cells in which you want to add a function. For example, select the cell below a column of cells that contain values you want to add together.

2. On the **Home** tab, in the **Macros** group, click **Table**, and then click **Function**.

3. In the **Function** dialog box, click the **Select the function to apply to the cells** list arrow, and then click the function you want to use.

4. Click **OK**.

Skills review

In this chapter, you learned how to:

- Download and install the Onetastic add-in

- Manage notebooks by using OneCalendar

- Manage pages and styles by using Onetastic

- Manage content, images, and tables by using Onetastic

Onetastic macros in OneNote

The additional capabilities that Onetastic brings to OneNote are made possible by *macros*, which are sections of executable programming code that instruct OneNote to perform simple repeated tasks. For example, rather than right-clicking and deleting every hyperlink on a page, you can use a macro included with Onetastic to remove the hyperlinks with a single button click.

Writing macros for OneNote is beyond the scope of this book, but you can find a large and growing collection of macros on the Macroland page of the Onetastic website. Macroland also contains programming resources to which you can refer if you want to write your own macros for OneNote.

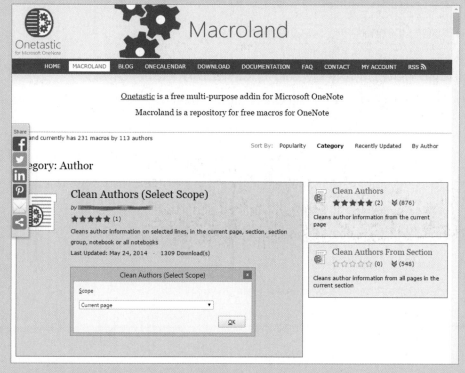

Find macros and macro resources for Onetastic

11

Practice tasks

The practice files for these tasks are located in the OneNoteSBS\Ch11 folder. The results of the tasks will be automatically saved into the same file in the same folder.

Download and install the Onetastic add-in

Start OneNote, and then perform the following tasks:

1. In OneNote, verify whether the version of the OneNote app on your computer is the 32-bit or 64-bit version.

2. In your web browser, go to *www.omeratay.com/onetastic/*, and then download the **Onetastic** installer.

3. Install **Onetastic** on your computer.

Manage notebooks by using OneCalendar

Open the ManageDates section in OneNote, and then perform the following tasks:

1. Open OneCalendar, and then display your notebook pages in month view.

2. Change your selected notebooks to only view your current notebook.

3. Go to November 2015 to see when the Project 97220 Offsite page was created.

4. Navigate among the months by using the tools available in OneCalendar.

5. Change your selected notebooks to view all the notebooks.

6. Change to weekly view.

7. View pages changed or created today.

Manage pages and styles by using Onetastic

Open the ManagePages section in OneNote, and then perform the following tasks:

1. Select the text *Proposed Location*, and then change its formatting.

2. Create a new custom style named **Subheader** based on the selected text.

3. Use the Onetastic buttons on the ribbon to add the current page as a favorite.

Manage content, images, and tables by using Onetastic

Open the ManageImages section in OneNote, and then perform the following tasks:

1. Use search and replace to change the word *Proposed* to **Possible**.

2. Resize the image so its height and width are **80** percent of its current size.

3. Create a formula in the *Total* row of the table to find the sum of the two values in the rightmost table column.

Keyboard shortcuts

This list of shortcuts is a comprehensive list derived from Microsoft OneNote Help. Some of the shortcuts might not be available in every version of OneNote.

Take and format notes

Type and edit notes

To do this	Press
Open a new OneNote window	Ctrl+M
Open a quick note (a small OneNote window) to create a side note	Ctrl+Shift+M or Windows logo key+Alt+N
Dock or undock the OneNote window	Ctrl+Alt+D
Undo the last action	Ctrl+Z
Redo the last action	Ctrl+Y
Select all items in the current line, note, or page (Press Ctrl+A more than once to increase the scope of the selection)	Ctrl+A
Cut the selected text or item	Ctrl+X
Copy the selected text or item to the Clipboard	Ctrl+C
Paste the contents of the Clipboard	Ctrl+V
Move to the beginning of the line	Home
Move to the end of the line	End
Move one character to the left	Left Arrow
Move one character to the right	Right Arrow
Move one word to the left	Ctrl+Left Arrow

To do this	Press
Move one word to the right	Ctrl+Right Arrow
Delete one character to the left	Backspace
Delete one character to the right	Delete
Delete one word to the left	Ctrl+Backspace
Delete one word to the right	Ctrl+Delete
Insert a line break without starting a new paragraph	Shift+Enter
Check spelling	F7
Open the thesaurus for the currently selected word	Shift+F7
Bring up the shortcut menu for any note, tab, or any other object that currently has focus	Shift+F10
Execute the action suggested on the Information Bar if it appears at the top of a page	Ctrl+Shift+W

Format notes

To do this	Press
Highlight selected text	Ctrl+Shift+H
Highlight or remove highlight from selected text	Ctrl+Alt+H
Insert a link using the selected words or object	Ctrl+K
Copy the formatting of selected text (Format Painter)	Ctrl+Shift+C
Paste the formatting to selected text (Format Painter)	Ctrl+Shift+V
Open a link (The cursor must be placed anywhere within the formatted link text)	Enter
Apply or remove bold formatting from the selected text	Ctrl+B

To do this	Press
Apply or remove italic formatting from the selected text	Ctrl+I
Apply or remove the underline from the selected text	Ctrl+U
Apply or remove strikethrough from the selected text	
Apply or remove superscript formatting from the selected text	Ctrl+Shift+Equal sign
Apply or remove subscript formatting from the selected text	Ctrl+Equal sign
Apply or remove bulleted list formatting from the selected paragraph	Ctrl+Period
Apply or remove numbered list formatting from the selected paragraph	Ctrl+/
Apply a Heading 1 style to the current note	Ctrl+Alt+1
Apply a Heading 2 style to the current note	Ctrl+Alt+2
Apply a Heading 3 style to the current note	Ctrl+Alt+3
Apply a Heading 4 style to the current note	Ctrl+Alt+4
Apply a Heading 5 style to the current note	Ctrl+Alt+5
Apply a Heading 6 style to the current note	Ctrl+Alt+6
Apply the Normal style to the current note	Ctrl+Shift+N
Indent a paragraph from the left	Alt+Shift+Right Arrow
Remove a paragraph indent from the left	Alt+Shift+Left Arrow
Right-align the selected paragraph	Ctrl+R
Left-align the selected paragraph	Ctrl+L
Increase the font size of selected text	Ctrl+Shift+>
Decrease the font size of selected text	Ctrl+Shift+<
Clear all formatting applied to the selected text	Ctrl+Shift+N
Show or hide rule lines on the current page	Ctrl+Shift+R

Add items to a page

To do this	Press
Insert a document or file on the current page	Alt+N, then F
Insert a document or file as a printout on the current page	Alt+N, then O
Show or hide document printouts on the current page (when running OneNote in High Contrast mode)	Alt+Shift+P
Insert a picture from a file	Alt+N, then P
Insert the current date	Alt+Shift+D
Insert the current date and time	Alt+Shift+F
Insert the current time	Alt+Shift+T
Insert a line break	Shift+Enter
Start a math equation or convert selected text to a math equation	Alt+Equal sign
Find the answer to a typed math equation	Enter the math equation, followed by an equal sign and a space
Insert a euro (€) symbol	Ctrl+Alt+E
Create a table by adding a second column to already typed text	Tab
Create another column in a table with a single row	Tab
Create another row when at the end cell of a table	Enter
Create a row below the current row in a table	Ctrl+Enter
Create another paragraph in the same cell in a table	Alt+Enter
Create a column to the right of the current column in a table	Ctrl+Alt+R
Create a row above the current one in a table (when the cursor is at the beginning of any row)	Enter
Delete the current empty row in a table (when the cursor is at the beginning of the row)	Delete (press twice)

Select notes and objects

To do this	Press
Select all items on the current page (when no notes are currently selected)	Ctrl+A
Select to the end of the line	Shift+End
Select the whole line (when the cursor is at the beginning of the line)	Shift+Down Arrow
Jump to the title of the page and select it	Ctrl+Shift+T
Cancel the selected outline or page	Esc
Move the current paragraph or selected paragraphs up	Alt+Shift+Up Arrow
Move the current paragraph or selected paragraphs down	Alt+Shift+Down Arrow
Move the current paragraph or selected paragraphs left (decreasing the indent)	Alt+Shift+Left Arrow
Move the current paragraph or selected paragraphs right (increasing the indent)	Alt+Shift+Right Arrow
Select the current paragraph and its subordinate paragraphs	Ctrl+Shift+Hyphen
Delete the selected note or object	Delete
Move to the beginning of the line	Home
Move to the end of the line	End
Move one character to the left	Left Arrow
Move one character to the right	Right Arrow
Go back to the last page visited	Alt+Left Arrow
Go forward to the next page visited	Alt+Right Arrow
Start playback of a selected audio or video recording	Ctrl+Alt+P or Ctrl+Alt+S
Rewind the current audio or video recording by a few seconds	Ctrl+Alt+Y
Fast-forward the current audio or video recording by a few seconds	Ctrl+Alt+U

Tag notes

To do this	Press
Apply, mark, or clear the To Do tag (or the first tag in the Tags gallery, if you added custom tags)	Ctrl+1
Apply or clear the Important tag (or the second tag in the Tags gallery)	Ctrl+2
Apply or clear the Question tag (or the third tag)	Ctrl+3
Apply or clear the Remember For Later tag (or the fourth tag)	Ctrl+4
Apply or clear the Definition tag (or the fifth tag)	Ctrl+5
Apply or clear the Highlight tag (or the sixth tag)	Ctrl+6
Apply or clear the Contact tag (or the seventh tag)	Ctrl+7
Apply or clear the Address tag (or the eighth tag)	Ctrl+8
Apply or clear the Phone Number tag (or the ninth tag)	Ctrl+9
Remove all note tags from the selected notes	Ctrl+0

Use outlines for indented text

To do this	Press
Show only Level 1 (hide indented text)	Alt+Shift+1
Expand to Level 2	Alt+Shift+2
Expand to Level 3	Alt+Shift+3
Expand to Level 4	Alt+Shift+4
Expand to Level 5	Alt+Shift+5
Expand to Level 6	Alt+Shift+6
Expand to Level 7	Alt+Shift+7
Expand to Level 8	Alt+Shift+8
Expand to Level 9	Alt+Shift+9
Expand all levels	Alt+Shift+0

To do this	Press
Increase indent by one level (select at least one character or the leftmost space of the line, to avoid creating a table)	Tab
Decrease indent by one level	Shift+Tab
Expand a collapsed outline	Alt+Shift+Plus sign
Collapse an expanded outline	Alt+Shift+Minus sign

Organize and manage your notebook

Work with pages and quick notes

To do this	Press
Enable or disable full-page view	F11
Open a new OneNote window	Ctrl+M
Open a small OneNote window to create a quick note	Ctrl+Shift+M
Expand or collapse the tabs of a page group (indented pages in the page tab pane)	Ctrl+Shift+*
Print the current page	Ctrl+P
Add a new page at the end of the selected section	Ctrl+N
Increase the width of the page tab pane	Ctrl+Shift+[
Decrease the width of the page tab pane	Ctrl+Shift+]
Create a new page below the current page tab at the same level	Ctrl+Alt+N
Decrease indent level of the current page tab label (as it appears in the page tab pane)	Ctrl+Alt+[
Increase indent level of the current page tab label	Ctrl+Alt+]
Create a new subpage below the current page	Ctrl+Shift+Alt+N

To do this	Press
Select all items	Ctrl+A (Press several times to increase the scope of the selection)
Select the current page	Ctrl+Shift+A
Move the selected page tab up (this action does not move child pages)	Alt+Shift+Up Arrow
Move the selected page tab down	Alt+Shift+Down Arrow
Move the cursor to the page title	Ctrl+Shift+T
Go to the first page in the currently visible set of page tabs	Alt+Page Up
Go to the last page in the currently visible set of page tabs	Alt+Page Down
Scroll up in the current page	Page Up
Scroll down in the current page	Page Down
Scroll to the top of the current page	Ctrl+Home
Scroll to the bottom of the current page	Ctrl+End
Go to the next paragraph	Ctrl+Down Arrow
Go to the previous paragraph	Ctrl+Up Arrow
Go to the next note container	Alt+Down Arrow
Go to the beginning of the line	Home
Go to the end of the line	End
Move one character to the left	Left Arrow
Move one character to the right	Right Arrow
Go back to the last page visited	Alt+Left Arrow
Go forward to the next page visited	Alt+Right Arrow
Zoom in	Alt+Ctrl+Plus sign (on the numeric keypad) or Alt+Ctrl+Shift+Plus sign
Zoom out	Alt+Ctrl+Minus sign (on the numeric keypad) or Alt+Ctrl+Shift+Hyphen

Work with notebooks and sections

To do this	Press
Open OneNote (if OneNote isn't open)	Windows logo key+Shift+N
Open a notebook	Ctrl+O
Open the OneNote Windows tool (the default behavior is to open a new quick note)	Windows logo key+N
Create a new section	Ctrl+T
Open a section file	Ctrl+Alt+Shift+O
Go to the next section	Ctrl+Tab
Go to the previous section	Ctrl+Shift+Tab
Go to the next page in the section	Ctrl+Page Down
Go to the previous page in the section	Ctrl+Page Up
Go to the first page in the section	Alt+Home
Go to the last page in the section	Alt+End
Go to the first page in the currently visible set of page tabs	Alt+Page Up
Go to the last page of the currently visible set of page tabs	Alt+Page Down
Move or copy the current page	Ctrl+Alt+M
Put focus on the current page tab	Ctrl+Alt+G
Select the current page tab	Ctrl+Shift+A
Put focus on the current section tab	Ctrl+Shift+G
Move the current section	Ctrl+Shift+G, and then Shift+F10, then M
Switch to a different notebook on the Navigation bar	Ctrl+G, then press Down Arrow or Up Arrow keys to select a different notebook, and then press Enter

Search notes

To do this	Press
Move the cursor to the Search box to search all notebooks	Ctrl+E
While searching all notebooks, preview the next result	Down Arrow
While searching all notebooks, go to the selected result and dismiss Search	Enter
Change the search scope	Ctrl+E, Tab, then Space
Open the Search Results pane	Alt+O after searching
Search only the current page	Ctrl+F
While searching the current page, move to the next result	Enter or F3
While searching the current page, move to the previous result	Shift+F3
Dismiss Search and return to the page	Esc

Share notes

Share notes with other people

To do this	Press
Send the selected pages in an email message	Ctrl+Shift+E

Share notes with other apps

To do this	Press
Create a Today Outlook task from the currently selected note	Ctrl+Shift+1
Create a Tomorrow Outlook task from the currently selected note	Ctrl+Shift+2
Create a This Week Outlook task from the currently selected note	Ctrl+Shift+3
Create a Next Week Outlook task from the currently selected note	Ctrl+Shift+4
Create a No Date Outlook task from the currently selected note	Ctrl+Shift+5
Open the selected Outlook task	Ctrl+Shift+K
Mark the selected Outlook task as complete	Ctrl+Shift+9
Sync changes in the current shared notebook	Shift+F9
Sync changes in all shared notebooks	F9
Mark the current page as Unread	Ctrl+Q

Password-protect sections

To do this	Press
Lock all password-protected sections	Ctrl+Alt+L

Index

O

About the author

Curtis Frye is the author of more than 30 books, including *Microsoft Excel 2016 Step by Step* for Microsoft Press and *Brilliant Excel VBA Programming* for Pearson, UK. He has also created and recorded more than three dozen courses for lynda.com, including *Tableau 9 Essential Training* and *Up and Running with Public Data Sets*. In addition to his work as a writer, Curt is a popular conference speaker and performer, both as a solo presenter and as part of the Portland, Oregon ComedySportz improvisational comedy troupe. He lives in Portland with his wife and three cats.

Acknowledgments

Creating a book is a team effort. And yes, I say "creating" rather than "writing." *Microsoft OneNote Step by Step*, as with all other books from Microsoft Press, required a team of professionals to shape raw materials provided by the author into a finished product that readers can rely on. First, thanks to Carol Dillingham for inviting me to be part of this team, and to Rosemary Caperton who brought me back for *Microsoft Excel 2016 Step by Step*. The team at OTSI included Kathy Krause, project editor and copy editor; Jeanne Craver, graphic artist; Susie Carr and Joan Lambert, desktop publishers and indexers; and Jaime Odell, proofreader.

I've left our technical reviewer, Ed Price, for last. Ed brought years of experience with OneNote to the project and, through his notes on my original text and his own contributions, helped transform this book into a resource that will benefit readers for years to come. I value his perspective and insights. His contributions, as with those of the other team members, might be invisible within the finished work, but they are there and I am grateful.

Now that you've read the book...

Tell us what you think!

Was it useful?
Did it teach you what you wanted to learn?
Was there room for improvement?

Let us know at http://aka.ms/tellpress

Your feedback goes directly to the staff at Microsoft Press,
and we read every one of your responses. Thanks in advance!

 Microsoft